While Reading Through John's Gospel
- 2 -

While Reading Through John's Gospel
- 2 -
B.E. Yoo
ISBN-13: 978-1-60668-008-7
ISBN-10: 1-60668-008-0
Copyright © 2007, Evangelical Media Group, Inc.
Printed in U.S.A.
No part of this book may be reproduced
without permission from the publisher.

While Reading Through John's Gospel
- 2 -

B.E. Yoo

Evangelical Media Group

◆ Explanatory Notes

1. The King James Version of the Bible is used in this book unless indicated otherwise.

2. This is the first of a series of books based on 55 sermons. (Originally, there were 56 sermons but two of them were combined as one.) Each sermon was originally about two hours long.

3. The speaker approached John's Gospel in chronological order, focusing each sermon on a specific passage.

4. After each sermon, the speaker and a team of editors spent time reviewing the content of the sermons.

◆ Foreword

While Reading Through John's Gospel

It might be said that John's Gospel focuses strongly on spiritual matters, and the other three Gospels present accounts of many of Jesus' teachings and physical activities. Matthew and Luke's Gospels, for example, contain detailed accounts of the events surrounding Jesus' birth, while John's Gospel does not even mention His birth.

John's Gospel, however, explains more powerfully than the other three Gospels what kind of personage Jesus was. The very first verse tells us, "In the beginning was the Word, and the Word was with God, and the Word was God" John 1:1. It announces precisely that Jesus was the Word that has existed from the beginning, and at the same time, He was God. So we might say that Matthew, Mark, and Luke's Gospels concentrate more on Jesus' physical actions, while John's Gospel focuses on Jesus' mind, in other words, His thoughts. In John chapter 20 verse 31, the apostle John expressed very clearly his purpose in writing this Gospel:

> "But these are written, that ye might believe that Jesus is the Christ, the Son of God; and that believing ye might have life through his name."

Also, in John chapter 5 verse 39 it says, "[You] Search the scriptures; for in them ye think ye have eternal life: and they are they which testify of me." The apostle John wrote that his reason for recording John's Gospel was so that we, as individuals, might have eternal life. The Bible is different from any other book in the world in that it deals with the matter of eternal life, that is, the matter of the human spirit. As we draw near to the Bible, we are able to examine matters that are related to our lives, and more specifically, our spirits. For this reason, when we read the Bible, it should be with the most sincere of hearts.

Which is the most precious book ever written in the history of mankind? People sometimes describe a piece of writing as being "a real gem" but is there any literary gem more precious than the words of the Bible? Aren't there times when a Bible verse that you have read many times before suddenly takes on a new meaning for you, giving you a peace in your spirit that nothing in this world could give to you?

There is no book that can compare to the Bible. When you read other books, they offer little more than the experience of climbing a bare mountain. The Bible, however, gives the reader that feeling of being deep in the mountains, eager to climb and explore. From a distance, all you may see is a mountain ridge, but the deeper you go in amongst the mountains, the more you discover: valley after valley, countless trees, streams, and rocks. The same is true of the Bible. No matter how many times you may read the Bible, it will seem different every time. The content remains the same, but each time you read it, you see it from a different perspective. So, when you approach the Bible, you should examine it thoroughly, bearing in mind that it is a real treasure.

The Bible describes the conception of the nation of Israel. The seed of this nation fell to the ground and as descendants were born, they were planted in the land that God had promised them. A nation was established in that land, that nation became stronger, and at times the members of that nation had to endure tremendous hardships. God called Abraham, the forefather of that nation, and commanded him, saying, "Get thee out of thy country, and from thy kindred, and from thy father's house, unto a land that I will shew thee" Genesis 12:1. Abraham put his trust in these words of God and set out on his journey. Later, he again believed God's words of promise and as a result, he was given a son, Isaac, to be his heir. Abraham's life continued step by step, just as it says in Romans chapter 1 verse 17: "For therein is the righteousness of God revealed from faith to faith." Little by little, the fellowship that Abraham had with God became deeper, as he advanced from faith to faith towards the land of Canaan. In our case, too, as we draw near to the Bible, we come to discover Jesus Christ, just as the Bible tells us: "So then faith cometh by hearing, and hearing by the word of God" Romans 10:17. Also, Jesus was born through the word of God. He came in accordance with the words of the Old Testament, and He died and rose again from the dead in accordance with these same words. This is why we also take pride in having been born of God's word. It is only through the words of the Bible that a person's spirit is born again. Doesn't the Bible say that God "begat ... us with the word of truth" James 1:18? Without God's word, we could not be born as citizens of the kingdom of God. This is why we need to keep close to the words of the Bible with childlike hearts and be able to look to Jesus Christ.

The words of the Bible are the words of God and they are as alive today as they were at the time of Abraham, the father of faith, and at any other time in history. Also, the words of the Bible wield the power to be able to take hold of the spirit and heart of any individual during their life in this world and guide them until they come to stand before the Lord. Since the One who has boarded the same boat as we are on has said, "Let us go over unto the other side" Luke 8:22, since He has determined our destination and His words are alive, we must not forget His words when we face the storms of this world.

The reason I am saying all this before we commence our study of John's Gospel is that I earnestly hope that through these studies, we may be able to come closer to God's word and thus be able to overcome the many worries, anxieties, and hardships of this world. All we need to do is allow God's word to be the light that guides us through our lives, as it says in the book of Psalms: "Thy word is a lamp unto my feet, and a light unto my path" Psalm 119:105.

When Peter looked to Jesus as He was walking on the water, Peter was also able to stand on the water. When a storm arose shortly after this, however, Peter looked at the waves with fear and began to sink. When we first came to know the gospel and believed firmly in the love of Jesus Christ, we floated above all the storms of the world. Our hearts definitely stood above the storm and were not pulled down into it. As we continue to live in this turbulent world, however, the time comes when we become aware that we are beginning to sink. Our lives become increasingly sluggish.

When Jesus came to this world and before He began His public ministry, He experienced something that was also intended as a lesson for us. As the devil tempted Him to turn some stones into bread, Jesus replied, "Man shall not live by bread alone, but by every word that proceedeth out of the mouth of God" See Matthew 4:3-4. He said these words at a time when He himself was suffering from extreme hunger.

Even though we know in theory that the words of the Bible are food for our spirits, if we are not careful, we may easily forget to apply these words to our actual lives. So as we deal with the matters of our lives in this world, we need to form a habit of using every spare moment to read the Bible so that whenever and wherever we sit down we think about reading the Bible.

In the Psalms it says, "Blessed is the man that walketh not in the counsel of the ungodly, nor standeth in the way of sinners, nor sitteth in the seat of the scornful. But his delight is in the law of the Lord; and in his law doth he meditate day and night" Psalm 1:1-2. As we are living in this world, we should always chew over God's word thoroughly and trust in His word in our hearts. Love is always a matter of give and take. We become aware of God's love through His word so shouldn't we also demonstrate our love for God by obeying His word in our lives?

The only truth is Jesus Christ who is in the Bible. If you do not know Jesus Christ, all you are doing is stepping on mere shadows of the truth. Jesus said, "I am the way, the truth, and the life: no man cometh unto the Father, but by me" John 14:6. There is no other way than this. So the Bible says, "There is a way which seemeth right unto a man, but the end thereof are the ways of death" Proverbs 14:12, and Jesus said, "Enter ye in at the strait gate" Matthew 7:13.

As you are reading the Bible, you may often find that verses come to mind other than the ones you are reading. There are many times when I am reading John's Gospel and other verses flash through my mind, so I look up these verses and read that part of the Bible for a while. Sometimes while I am reading John's Gospel, I turn to the book of Jeremiah and read that, or Isaiah, or Genesis. This is because I find I understand John's Gospel better by reading these other books as well. The mysteries of the Bible are only unraveled by other passages from the Bible.

The apostle John actually met and touched the One who was the Word. There was something that he knew for certain. This was why he wrote, "That which was from the beginning, which we have heard, which we have seen with our eyes, which we have looked upon, and our hands have handled, of the Word of life" 1 John 1:1. It is the testimony of this apostle John that we read in John's Gospel. Through John's Gospel, the apostle testifies as to who Jesus Christ was. Who is this Jesus in whom we believe? It is the Jesus that appears in John's Gospel.

The content of John's Gospel is of a higher dimension. It deals with magnificent and grandiose matters, not of this earth but of heaven above. So, as we study John's Gospel, we may see this as a time to lay ourselves a firm foundation in God's word. Once we have finished a thorough study of John's Gospel, it will probably be easier to understand other parts of the Bible.

We should see our studies of John's Gospel as an opportunity to be able to understand the Bible more easily; we should not think that once we have studied John's Gospel there will be no need to study the Bible any more. There is in fact no end to studying the Bible. It is my hope that those who hear and read the content of this book will see in it not the writer, but Jesus Christ alone. I also hope that His words and His words alone remain in the hearts and minds of my readers.

◆ Index

8	Except a Man Be Born Again John 3:1-15	15
9	For God So Loved The World John 3:16-21	49
10	He Must Increase But I Must Decrease John 3:22-4:2	89
11	Living Water that Quenches Spiritual Thirst John 4:3-19	117
12	The Essential Nature of Worship and the Eternal Harvest John 4:20-42	137

13	The Appropriate Response to Faith John 4:43-54	171
14	The True Sabbath: Eternal Rest John 5:1-18	183
15	Eternal Life and Eternal Punishment John 5:19-29	213
16	Why Read the Bible? John 5:30-47	237
◆	Notes	258

8

Except a Man Be Born Again

John 3:1-15

If the Bible had not said, "Ye must be born again,"
Christianity would put more of a burden on its followers
than any religion in the world.
Being born again does not require
any activity or righteousness on man's part.
It is a matter of a seed of life beginning to grow.

John 3:1-15

[1]There was a man of the Pharisees, named Nicodemus, a ruler of the Jews: [2]The same came to Jesus by night, and said unto him, Rabbi, we know that thou art a teacher come from God: for no man can do these miracles that thou doest, except God be with him.

[3]Jesus answered and said unto him, Verily, verily, I say unto thee, Except a man be born again, he cannot see the kingdom of God.

[4]Nicodemus saith unto him, How can a man be born when he is old? can he enter the second time into his mother's womb, and be born?

[5]Jesus answered, Verily, verily, I say unto thee, Except a man be born of water and of the Spirit, he cannot enter into the kingdom of God. [6]That which is born of the flesh is flesh; and that which is born of the Spirit is spirit. [7]Marvel not that I said unto thee, Ye must be born again. [8]The wind bloweth where it listeth, and thou hearest the sound thereof, but canst not tell whence it cometh, and whither it goeth: so is every one that is born of the Spirit.

[9]Nicodemus answered and said unto him, How can these things be?

[10]Jesus answered and said unto him, Art thou a master of Israel, and knowest not these things? [11]Verily, verily, I say unto thee, We speak that we do know, and testify that we have seen; and ye receive not our witness. [12]If I have told you earthly things, and ye believe not, how shall ye believe, if I tell you of heavenly things? [13]And no man hath ascended up to heaven, but he that came down from heaven, even the Son of man which is in heaven. [14]And as Moses lifted up the serpent in the wilderness, even so must the Son of man be lifted up: [15]That whosoever believeth in him should not perish, but have eternal life.

Ye Must Be Born Again

I often wonder what kind of religion Christianity would have become if the Bible had not said, "Ye must be born again" John 3:7. Without these words, Christianity would put more of a burden on its followers than any religion in the world. Trying to keep the Ten Commandments and the many other laws recorded in the Old Testament would turn Christianity into a religion that would impose a tremendous stress on the individual.

However, Jesus said, "Come unto me, all ye that labour and are heavy laden, and I will give you rest" Matthew 11:28. Christianity is distinguished from all the religions of the world in that it requires that the individual be born again. A path different from any religion has been opened as a result of the experience of being born again.

The media often speak in their news reports of the "rebirth," or the "saving" of society. They talk of the need for society to be renewed or of the need for the rebirth of some organization or government. Much is said of the need to save society, but the need for the salvation of the individual is not a popular topic of discussion.

Despite all the cries for the rebirth of society, it cannot actually be born again. All anyone can really do is make resolutions and plans. This is far from the rebirth of the individual that is dealt with in the Bible. What happens when you try to apply this phenomenon to society? Can an organization, nation, corporation, or any such group be born again? People cannot really do much more than cry out for reform.

These words that Jesus addressed to one particular individual regarding the need to be born again are very important. If it had not been for this message, Christians would be better off not believing or doing anything at all. When we look back over the two-thousand-year history of Christianity and consider the efforts made by

Christians during that time, we find that that history would have been no more than a scene of confusion and disorder if it had not been for the belief in the experience of being born again. There have been the conflicts between the Catholic and Protestant Churches, the matter of selling indulgences[1] and various other problems within the Catholic Church. Then there have been the struggles between the different Protestant denominations. It cannot be denied that the two-thousand-year history of Christianity, including both the Catholic and Protestant Churches, has been complicated and tumultuous.

Fortunately, however, Jesus told us to "Enter ... in at the strait gate" Matthew 7:13, and John chapter 3 explains the process by which a person can do this, in other words, the process of being born again. This is a very important message and it contains a warning for all the people in this world who follow some form of religion, all who are looking for some kind of god, and all who try to live good and pure lives.

Being born again does not require any activity or righteousness on man's part, and neither is there a price to pay for it. There is no need for any course of academic study either. What does it mean to be born? When a chick hatches from an egg, it does not make a conscious effort to do so. A chick does not learn to become a chick; a seed of life simply develops within the egg. Life does not come about through education, ideologies, or training; it begins as a seed that develops and is born. The cultivation of moral standards, hard work, or good deeds are not required in order for life to come into being.

There are probably people who sometimes ask themselves, "Of all the countries in this world, why did I have to be born in one like this?" There are also probably people who say, "I don't know why I bother to live in a world full of so much evil." Some people are probably dissatisfied with their country even though it boasts of a highly developed culture, while others long for their homeland, lost to them through troubles and turmoil.

When the Bible talks about being born again, however, it has nothing to do with the country in which a person is born, or being born in a mountain village or a highly civilized town. This is something that goes beyond physical birth; it is a case of being born into the realms of true life. John chapter 3 strongly emphasizes this requirement.

Nicodemus Came to Jesus

A man named Nicodemus came to see Jesus at night. At that time, Jesus was closely watched by the public eye, and the religious leaders followed His every move. Some people have speculated that Nicodemus came to Jesus by night out of consideration for his own personal safety and to avoid being seen and having people associate him with this infamous Man. Others suggest that perhaps it was because he had to consider his position and reputation as a religious leader and scholar of the law.

Nicodemus, however, was not such a coward. If we read through the New Testament, we can see that he comes across as a man who had no time for fear. He had such courage and was so full of conviction that he was even bold in rebuking those who were criticizing Jesus and were ready to hand Him over for execution. As a result, he came under attack himself.

Let's turn to John chapter 7.

"Then came the officers to the chief priests and Pharisees; and they said unto them, Why have ye not brought him? The officers answered, Never man spake like this man. Then answered them the

Pharisees, Are ye also deceived? Have any of the rulers or of the Pharisees believed on him? But this people who knoweth not the law are cursed." John 7:45-49

The Pharisees sent officers to investigate and seize Jesus, but rather than laying hands on Him, they came back, having been moved by His words. So the Pharisees said, "Have any of the rulers or of the Pharisees believed on him?" John 7:48. They attempted to make a display of their authority, pointing out that amongst the Pharisees, the most orthodox sect of the Jews and the greatest scholars of the Scriptures, there were none who believed in Jesus. The Pharisees also criticized Jesus and His disciples, accusing them of having broken the laws of the Sabbath. Jesus' disciples had picked some heads of grain and eaten them on the Sabbath day, and Jesus Himself had healed the sick on this day. Therefore the leaders of the Jews accused them of not knowing the law and said they were cursed. At that time,

> "Nicodemus saith unto them, (he that came to Jesus by night, being one of them,) Doth our law judge any man, before it hear him, and know what he doeth?" John 7:50-51

When Nicodemus heard the words of the chief priests and Pharisees, he became indignant. When we consider instances such as this, we can see that Nicodemus was not a man who would have come to Jesus by night because he was afraid of what others might think of him. He, too, was a teacher of Israel who was well versed in the Scriptures. At the time of the crucifixion when the air was thick with unrest, this brave man came with Joseph of Arimathea to collect Jesus' body and anoint it with fragrant oils.[2]

We can see that Nicodemus was more than an ordinary man. He was not a person to sneak around by night to make sure that no one saw him. In certain respects, his character comes across in sharp contrast to that of Peter who followed Jesus around for three years and then denied Him three times, saying, "I know not the man." Nicodemus was a fearless individual who would submit to no one.

Nicodemus and Jesus

Such was the character of this man who came to Jesus by night. The meeting that took place that night is the most important meeting in human history. We know of many great figures who have appeared in the history of mankind, and their biographies have been written out in full for all to read. The Bible only makes brief mention of Nicodemus, but it seems to me that his conversation with Jesus that night was the single most important conversation that has ever taken place.

As a scholar of the Scriptures, Nicodemus had been watching Jesus and the deeds He had performed, and they had given him food for thought. He had sensed that there was something deeply significant to all of this and so he came to see Jesus. He had come to the conclusion that this Man must have come down from heaven or He would never have been able to act with such daring. So he decided to come and speak with Jesus. He sought out this great Teacher in order to ask Him about a matter that concerned his whole being.

This man who would submit to no one was speaking as a teacher of Israel as he stood before Jesus and said, "Having seen the things You do, I'm certain You must have come from heaven."

Let's try to imagine this scene. These two men were meeting for the first time. Nicodemus had come to Jesus with the greatest question of his whole life, but Jesus began to give him an answer that had nothing to do with this question. In fact, He told Nicodemus that there was something that he had to do.

If we consider the backgrounds of Nicodemus and Jesus, we can see that there was a tremendous difference between these two men. Nicodemus was a member of the Council of the Jews. He was a scholar, thoroughly versed in the law. But what kind of person was Jesus? Even His birth had not taken place in a proper human dwelling; He had been born in a stable. In the eyes of the world, He was "(as was supposed) the son of Joseph" Luke 3:23. In terms of His social status, He had grown up in the family of a carpenter.

Once Jesus had turned thirty, He began to appear in public and carry out His work. It was then that Nicodemus, this highly educated scholar of the law, came to see Him. How do you think Jesus saw Nicodemus at that time? For Jesus, this was not a meeting, man to man, between a great scholar and a religious leader. Nicodemus had eagerly awaited the coming of the Messiah. He had searched the Scriptures to find out all he could about Him, and he had even taught about Him. Now the Messiah he had sought for so long was standing in front of him talking to him, but He was quite different from the Person he had been expecting. Jesus did not regard Nicodemus with any form of human love, sympathy, or emotion; His words were full of the power of the One who is the very source of mercy. This was not a discussion between two religious leaders, two scholars of the law, two people who understood the Old Testament scriptures and the words of the prophets. This was not an exchange of ideas between equals. Jesus' words were full of a tremendous compassion for this man who had come in search of something. Through whose eyes was Jesus looking at him?

Except a Man Be Born Again

"There was a man of the Pharisees, named Nicodemus, a ruler of the Jews: The same came to Jesus by night, and said unto him, Rabbi, we know that thou art a teacher come from God: for no man can do these miracles that thou doest, except God be with him." John 3:1-2

Nicodemus said he was certain that Jesus was a teacher come from God. He knew that no one could have done these signs that Jesus did unless God was with him. He was convinced of this. These words were extremely important. Jesus' answer, however, had nothing to do with what Nicodemus had said; He began to talk about something completely different.

"Jesus answered and said unto him, Verily, verily, I say unto thee, Except a man be born again, he cannot see the kingdom of God." John 3:3

These words that Jesus addressed to Nicodemus were unlike anything that might come up in an ordinary everyday conversation from one person to another. Jesus was talking about something that man had lost at the very beginning when he had first been created. Nicodemus had studied and matured to a standard that qualified him as a ruler of the Jews. As a teacher, he was a very knowledgeable man, and this knowledge that he had gained from his ancestors and the people around him gave him a certain authority. But Jesus said to him:

"Verily, verily, I say unto thee, Except a man be born again, he cannot see the kingdom of God."

These words related back to something that had happened in the beginning at the time of Adam. God put the responsibility on Adam when He told him not to eat the fruit of the tree of the knowledge of good and evil and said to him, "For in the day that thou eatest thereof thou shalt surely die" Genesis 2:17. But Adam disobeyed God and sinned, and when he did this, he lost something. There was something that he could have received, but the moment he sinned, he lost it. What was it that Adam lost?

"And the Lord God formed man of the dust of the ground, and breathed into his nostrils the breath of life; and man became a living soul. And the Lord God planted a garden eastward in Eden; and there he put the man whom he had formed. And out of the ground made the Lord God to grow every tree that is pleasant to the sight, and good for food; the tree of life also in the midst of the garden, and the tree of knowledge of good and evil." Genesis 2:7-9

It says that in the midst of the garden there were both the tree of life and the tree of the knowledge of good and evil. Which of the two did Adam chose? We all know—as the Pharisee, Nicodemus, also knew—that Adam chose the fruit of the tree of knowledge. But what had God said to Adam before he ate this fruit?

"And the Lord God took the man, and put him into the garden of Eden to dress it and to keep it. And the Lord God commanded the man, saying, Of every tree of the garden thou mayest freely eat: But of the tree of the knowledge of good and evil, thou shalt not eat of it: for in the day that thou eatest thereof thou shalt surely die." Genesis 2:15-17

God told Adam that he could eat the fruit of every tree in the garden except for that of the tree of knowledge. This means that he was also permitted to eat the fruit of the tree of life, doesn't it? God said, "Of every tree of the garden thou mayest freely eat," but then He made one restriction:

"But of the tree of the knowledge of good and evil, thou shalt not eat of it."

In spite of God's words, Adam ate the forbidden fruit. God had said, "For in the day that thou eatest thereof thou shalt surely die," and sure enough, as soon as Adam ate the fruit, he died. This was not a death that meant the end of his physical life; it meant that the communication between man and God was cut off. Adam could no longer remain in the Garden of Eden and he was cast out.

How should we understand this death that Adam experienced? If you cut some branches from a tree, the leaves on them will remain green for a while, but eventually they will wither and die. It is only a matter of time. The same is true of man. Adam ate the fruit of the tree of the knowledge of good and evil, and after that descendants were born to him. All of mankind are the descendants of Adam. Before we came into the world, Nicodemus was also born as a descendant of Adam. Ever since the forefather of all mankind received that death penalty, all of his descendants have slowly been walking the path to death.

What was this death that came to Adam? He was driven out of the Garden of Eden and cut off from all communication with God. The death that we associate with the decay of the flesh came later.

"And you hath he quickened, who were dead in trespasses and sins."

Ephesians 2:1

We who were dead in Adam have been made alive in Jesus.

The Kingdom of God

What did Jesus tell Nicodemus?

"You must be born again. I am telling you, you must be born again. Unless you are born again, you cannot see the kingdom of God."

One nineteenth-century believer wrote the following hymn to express his experience of being born again.

> Since Christ my soul from sin set free,
> This world has been a heav'n to me;
> And 'mid earth's sorrows and its woe,
> 'Tis heav'n my Jesus here to know.

> O hallelujah, yes, 'tis heaven,
> 'Tis heav'n to know my sins forgiv'n;
> On land or sea, what matters where?
> Where Jesus is, 'tis heaven there.[3]

> Where Jesus is, 'tis heaven there.

Once someone came to see me and she sang this hymn:

> Since Christ my soul from sin set free.

She did not seem to understand the true meaning of what she was singing, so to make it a little clearer, I asked her to put on her coat. When it was on, I asked her to take it off again. She took it off and once more I asked her to put it on.

"You notice a difference, don't you?" I said.

It was a cold day, and she said that she definitely did feel a difference between when she was wearing the coat and when she was not. So I told her:

"Once you realize the love of God, you know with absolute certainty whether or not you are clothed in His grace."

And so we began to talk about the Bible. A few days later, that woman sang the same hymn for me again but this time with the assurance that she, too, had become a child of God. This is what happens when an individual comes to realize the truth of the gospel.

Let's turn now to Luke's Gospel chapter 17.

"And Jesus answering said, Were there not ten cleansed? but where are the nine? There are not found that returned to give glory to God, save this stranger. And he said unto him, Arise, go thy way: thy faith hath made thee whole. And when he was demanded of the Pharisees, when the kingdom of God should come, he answered them and said,

The kingdom of God cometh not with observation: Neither shall they say, Lo here! or, lo there! for, behold, the kingdom of God is within you." Luke 17:20-21

In answer to the Pharisees' question, Jesus said, "Neither shall they say, Lo here! or, lo there!" Where did He say the kingdom of God is? He said it is "within you," in other words, it arises in your heart. Jesus was already there, moving around in the midst of the Pharisees. The kingdom of God had actually come upon them. The Pharisees knew the Old Testament scriptures, but their eyes were veiled, preventing them from seeing the truth. Jesus once said to His disciples, "These are the words which I spake unto you, … that all things must be fulfilled, which were written in the law of Moses, and in the prophets, and in the psalms, concerning me" Luke 24:44, and He then proceeded to explain the Scriptures to them. Those who already know the Bible only have one more step to take in order to come to the moment of realization and for the truth to arise in their hearts. This is what Jesus was saying.

This was also the case for Nicodemus as Jesus spoke to him.

"Verily, verily, I say unto thee, Except a man be born again."

In Romans chapter 5 it says that through the sin of one man, Adam, all of mankind became sinners, but through the righteousness of one Man, Jesus Christ, all have been made righteous. It explains how those who are dead in Adam are made alive in Jesus. What does all this mean? Let's consider here the fundamental nature of God, the Creator of the heaven and the earth.

> "In the beginning God created the heaven and the earth. And the earth was without form, and void; and darkness was upon the face of the deep. And the Spirit of God moved upon the face of the waters. And God said, Let there be light: and there was light. And God saw the light, that it was good: and God divided the light from the darkness."
>
> Genesis 1:1-5

Darkness absolutely needs light. The light of the sun, the moon, the stars, and all the other lights in this world exist merely as a shadow of a much greater, more brilliant and perfect light that will appear in the future.

Men's hearts dwell in the darkness that surrounds them. It was in the midst of this darkness that Nicodemus sought the true light. The Jews built their temple, and in it they placed the table for the showbread and they lit the candlestick. They installed the ark of the covenant in the Most Holy Place and there they sprinkled the blood of the sacrificial animals, but all of this was merely a shadow of something else. All these ceremonies were given as an example of what was to come and served only until they found the true light. Just as animals and insects are drawn to the light, man also seeks the light that will shine in his heart. This was the light that Nicodemus sought when he came to Jesus.

> "The spirit of man is the candle of the Lord, searching all the inward parts of the belly."
> Proverbs 20:27

> "Thy word is a lamp unto my feet, and a light unto my path."
> Psalm 119:105

When these words are accomplished in the heart of an individual, he will find the light by following the Lord's word. Every year the Jews came from Persia to the north, from Ethiopia and Egypt to the south, from Greece, from Rome and from wherever else in the world they had been scattered. They came to the temple in Jerusalem to bask in God's light. This temple, however, was no more than a shadow of the body of Jesus Christ.

The Temple of His Body

The body of Jesus Christ was torn and He shed His blood on the cross, but what was the significance of all this? In Old Testament times, the Israelites would shed the blood of sacrificial animals in the temple or transfer their sins to a scapegoat that would be released out in the wilderness. All of these procedures came to an end from the moment Jesus said, "It is finished," as He hung, dying on the cross.

Jesus said, "Destroy this temple, and in three days I will raise it up" John 2:19. This was the temple that Nicodemus had come to find—the true temple, the culmination of all the feasts of the Jews, the body of Jesus. All the teachers of the Jews who guided others toward this temple through the Old Testament scriptures also gathered in the temple. The temple and all the ceremonies carried out there were a model, a shadow of the true essence that was to come.

In Hebrews chapter 9 we have a brief explanation of all the sacrificial rites of the Jews. Let's turn to that chapter now.

> "For if the blood of bulls and of goats, and the ashes of an heifer sprinkling the unclean, sanctifieth to the purifying of the flesh: How much more shall the blood of Christ, who through the eternal Spirit offered himself without spot to God, purge your conscience from dead works to serve the living God?" Hebrews 9:13-14

Even the blood of the animals sacrificed each year could cleanse the sinner, so won't the eternal blood of Christ be able so much more to cleanse your conscience from dead works to serve the living God? Will His blood not be able to revive man's spirit that died when Adam sinned? The Bible tells us that the blood of the sacrificial animals was a shadow of the blood of Christ.

> "But Christ being come an high priest of good things to come, by a greater and more perfect tabernacle, not made with hands, that is to say, not of this building." Hebrews 9:11

There was to be a greater more perfect tabernacle, not made with hands. Christ had to be destroyed and killed for the sake of this great temple that He would accomplish in the future. It is also for the sake of this perfect temple that the believers on this earth continue to have fellowship with one another through the Spirit of Christ. Thus the temple is being built up.

In the future, when we go to the kingdom of God, we will see Christ and then we will understand that He Himself is the perfect temple. Nicodemus had not come to meet an ordinary man. Nicodemus was not aware of it at the time, but Jesus was speaking to him in order to invite him into this perfect temple.

> "It was therefore necessary that the patterns of things in the heavens should be purified with these; but the heavenly things themselves with better sacrifices than these. For Christ is not entered into the holy places made with hands, which are the figures of the true; but into heaven itself, now to appear in the presence of God for us."
>
> Hebrews 9:23-24

Now is not the time for the offering of the blood of animals. The apostle Paul once wrote of offering a living sacrifice that is acceptable to God, the sacrifice that we make when we serve other believers and guide others to salvation.[4] The time will come when the believers will meet the Lord as they stand before Him. It is when we see this perfect temple that we will meet Jesus.

When Jesus said, "Destroy this temple," He was not referring to the temple that had taken the Jews 46 years to build. He was speaking of the temple of His body that was soon to die. The apostle John wrote, "But he spake of the temple of his body. When therefore he was risen from the dead, his disciples remembered that he had said this unto them; and they believed the scripture, and the word which Jesus had said" John 2:21-22. Not even the disciples knew what Jesus meant when He said these words.

The Lamb Is Its Temple

Let's take a look now at what the Bible says about the eternal heavenly kingdom that is to come.

"And I saw a new heaven and a new earth: for the first heaven and the first earth were passed away; and there was no more sea. And I John saw the holy city, new Jerusalem, coming down from God out of heaven, prepared as a bride adorned for her husband. And I heard a great voice out of heaven saying, Behold, the tabernacle of God is with men, and he will dwell with them, and they shall be his people, and God himself shall be with them, and be their God. And God shall wipe away all tears from their eyes; and there shall be no more death, neither sorrow, nor crying, neither shall there be any more pain: for the former things are passed away. And he that sat upon the throne said, Behold, I make all things new. And he said unto me, Write: for these words are true and faithful. And he said unto me, It is done. I am Alpha and Omega, the beginning and the end. I will give unto him that is athirst of the fountain of the water of life freely. He that overcometh shall inherit all things; and I will be his God, and he shall be my son."
Revelation 21:1-7

"And he carried me away in the spirit to a great and high mountain, and shewed me that great city, the holy Jerusalem, descending out of heaven from God."
Revelation 21:10

There is a hymn that begins with the lines:

> Jerusalem, my happy home!
> Name ever dear to me.[5]

"Jerusalem, my happy home." What is to be found in this Jerusalem? The temple of God is there. John wrote that he saw the new Jerusalem coming down out of heaven, but we do not yet have a description of the temple within that city.

Revelation chapter 21 describes this perfect and eternal heavenly kingdom as having inexpressible beauty, being adorned with every kind of precious stone, sapphire, emerald, and amethyst, amongst others and its streets being paved with pure gold. John also wrote that there were no lamps in the city. Does that mean that it was dark? If it had been dark there, it could not have been the heavenly kingdom. There were no lights and yet John wrote that the city was bright.

> We shall stand, robed in white,
> In the bright and shining home,
> In eternal light.[6]

Heaven is a truly bright and shining home. Now let's turn to Revelation chapter 21 verse 22.

> "And I saw no temple therein: for the Lord God Almighty and the Lamb are the temple of it."

Who does it say is the temple? The temple that had taken 46 years to build was just a shadow of the true temple. Now, however, in the new Jerusalem, there are no more shadows since Jesus Himself is the temple. For as long as the believers are on this earth, the Church that is the body of Jesus Christ is the temple.

> "Know ye not that ye are the temple of God, and that the Spirit of God dwelleth in you?" 1 Corinthians 3:16

> "What? know ye not that your body is the temple of the Holy Ghost which is in you, which ye have of God, and ye are not your own?"
> 1 Corinthians 6:19

This is what the Bible says, isn't it? And this is what we believe.

> I'm rejoicing night and day,
> As I walk the pilgrim way,
> ...

> Yes, the secret all is this:
> That the Comforter abides with me.[7]

The Comforter, that is, the Spirit of the Lord, abides with each of us as individuals. When we enter the eternal heavenly kingdom, we will not be able to see a temple, since Jesus Himself is the perfect temple. It is through the Lamb of God that we see the temple.

> "And the city had no need of the sun, neither of the moon, to shine in it: for the glory of God did lighten it, and the Lamb is the light thereof."
> Revelation 21:23

There is no need for any other lights in this city because Jesus Himself is the light.

> "And there shall be no night there; and they need no candle, neither light of the sun; for the Lord God giveth them light: and they shall reign for ever and ever."
> Revelation 22:5

Now we have some idea of what the eternal heavenly kingdom is like. John looked for a lamp, and there was none. He looked for the temple, and could not find it. But the true temple was there. It is only when we actually go to the eternal heavenly kingdom that we will really know what it is like.

When By His Grace I Shall Look On His Face

One astronaut went up into space and said that there was no God there. The universe is so enormous, I wonder if even the scientists can truly estimate just how big it is. The heavens are so deep and wide, but is that the heaven that the Bible is talking about? When we talk about going to the heavenly kingdom, you might imagine that it is a very long way away and you would have to travel miles and miles to get there. But let's think about this.

> His perfect salvation, His wonderful love,
> I'll shout with the millions on high.[8]

On that day of perfect salvation, our bodies will be completely changed. What happened when Jesus' body underwent this transformation? His followers were worried and confused as they gathered behind locked doors to mourn the loss of their Teacher, and then suddenly He appeared in their midst. Thomas was not with them at the time, and later when they told him that they had seen the Lord, he said, "I will not believe unless I put my hand into His side where He was pierced."

Thomas wanted to believe Jesus with his fingers. He wanted to touch Jesus' wounded side with his hand. But then Jesus suddenly appeared amongst the disciples as they were gathered behind closed doors. Can you imagine this scene? What will it be like on the day when we experience this complete salvation and we are physically transformed to receive perfect bodies?

In the past it might have taken a month or more for a letter to be delivered by hand from New York to Chicago, and you could never be sure if it would actually arrive. That was the way people lived back then. If a neighbor moved away or a child got married and moved to another state, there would be little hope of ever seeing them again. It took such a long time to travel any great distance.

But life is very different these days; now you can make a telephone call:

"Mom! How are you doing?"

"I'm just fine. I'll be over to see you this afternoon."

In today's world, we can communicate within seconds. Life has become much faster. The prophet Daniel said, "Many shall run to and fro, and knowledge shall be increased" Daniel 12:4, and this is exactly how things are today. It is as though the Far East is right next door. Someone in New York can call a friend in Tokyo and reach him in an instant. In a similar way, when we go to the kingdom of God, the moment the Lord calls us, we will be right beside Him. Other people will probably be very surprised at that time. We will just disappear without even making a hole in the ceiling. In a moment in time, our thoughts and everything about us will suddenly be taken up out of this world.

Right now, we are living within the confines of time as it flows along, so it takes time for us to move from one place to another. God, on the other hand, is Lord over this hour, the next hour, and the hour that has just passed, over one end of space and the other. He said, "I am Alpha and Omega." We are restricted by time and space, but God is not limited by anything. On the day when we stand before this God, the kingdom of God will stretch right out before us. Such is the kingdom of God toward which we are heading.

> Friends will be there I have loved long ago;
> Joy like a river around me will flow;
> Yet, just a smile from my Saviour, I know,
> Will through the ages be glory for me.
> O that will be glory for me,
> Glory for me, glory for me;
> When by His grace I shall look on His face,
> That will be glory, be glory for me.[9]

When the kingdom of God opens before us like this, we will look on the face of the Lord.

It was this same Lord Jesus, the perfect temple, that Nicodemus met on that evening. He met face to face on this earth with the One who is perfect and had come from eternity.

Except a Man Be Born of Water and of the Spirit

> "Nicodemus saith unto him, How can a man be born when he is old? can he enter the second time into his mother's womb, and be born? Jesus answered, Verily, verily, I say unto thee, Except a man be born of water and of the Spirit, he cannot enter into the kingdom of God."
>
> John 3:4-5

Various people have had a great deal to say about the meaning of "water" and "the Spirit" in this verse. Some people claim that "water" here means the water used in baptism. If you examine the general flow of the Bible, however, it becomes clear that being "born of water" means being born again by the word of God. Those who heard John the Baptist preaching repented in their hearts and were baptized. This was the baptism of repentance. We should see this as indicating that once a person has been through this process of repentance, the Holy Spirit enters his spirit.

In verse 3 it says that unless a person is born again he cannot see the kingdom of God, and here in verse 5 it says that without being born again, a person cannot enter the kingdom of God. It says, "Except a man be born again, he cannot see the kingdom of God." First, a person comes to know the kingdom of God when he is born again during his life in this world. Then, he enters the kingdom of God when his body is changed into a perfect body. It is not just anyone who is able to enter the gates of the kingdom of God; only those who have been born again can enter them. When we say that we see the kingdom of God, it means that we have come to believe in Jesus while living in this world; as our spirits were born again we experienced the kingdom of God and our spirits have already entered in there. Each person who is born again, thus becoming a child of God, is a citizen of the kingdom of God.

The perfect kingdom of God, however, has not yet become a physical reality in this world. It is simply that, as we live in this world, we look forward to the eternal kingdom of blessing as it has been promised to us. In the not-so-distant future, when our bodies are perfectly transformed, we will enter the kingdom of God. When Jesus comes again, all the believers will enter the kingdom of God. Until then, our spirits will enjoy the righteousness and peace of God, but our bodies must live in this world and go through many difficulties, as it says in the Bible, "We must through much tribulation enter into the kingdom of God" Acts 14:22.

Some people claim to have seen the kingdom of God with their own eyes. They say that while they were praying they saw some kind of brilliant light. The kingdom of God, however, must be seen through the eyes of the heart. In the letter to the Ephesians, Paul wrote, "The eyes of your understanding being enlightened" Ephesians 1:18. When you are feeling dismal and frustrated and everything seems to be going wrong, and suddenly a good friend turns up, what happens to your face? It becomes more cheerful, doesn't it? Your heart brightens because somehow it is on the same wavelength as that of your friend. The true light is reflected in this same way.

> "That which is born of the flesh is flesh; and that which is born of the Spirit is spirit. Marvel not that I said unto thee, Ye must be born again." John 3:6-7

Jesus said, "Marvel not." In other words, do not think this is strange. "That which is born of the flesh is flesh." To put it simply, all those who are born of the seed of Adam are descendants of Adam. All of mankind has inherited the blood of Adam and therefore all are sinners. It is not a matter of how much a person has studied the Bible or whether he has studied or even taught theology. That is not the way for a person to enter the kingdom of God; a person must be born again. We are born in the flesh, but our spirits must be renewed. In other words, we must be changed. We must be born again.

> Ev'rything is changed since my sins were forgiven,
> Ev'rything is changed since I knew the Lord;
> Now my feet are walking the pathway to heaven;
> All the guilty past now is under the blood.
>
> Ev'rything is changed, praise the Lord!
> Now I am redeemed thro' the blood:
> Free from condemnation, God is my salvation,
> Ev'rything is changed, praise the Lord![10]

On one occasion, Peter, too, had a glimpse of the light of heaven and he said to Jesus:

"Thou art the Christ, the Son of the living God." Matthew 16:16

These words of Peter were far different from those of Nicodemus. Peter was simple and uneducated, but when the Spirit of God came upon him, there was no comparison between his words and those of Nicodemus, the scholar who had studied the Scriptures all his life. Just for a moment, Peter had heard the voice of God deep down in his spirit. In other words, he had seen the true light and his words were a reflection of that light.

On the other hand, how did Nicodemus see Jesus? He said:

"Rabbi, we know that thou art a teacher come from God: for no man can do these miracles that thou doest, except God be with him."

John 3:2

This scholar and teacher of the Scriptures was simply acknowledging the presence of a certain power from God that was beyond his own sphere of understanding and that he was ready to submit to this power.

Nicodemus had been groping around in the dark, waiting patiently. Then he had made up his mind that he just had to meet this Man and so he came to see Jesus. Nicodemus' words were very refined, but if you compare them with the words of the uneducated Peter, you can see that his eyes had not yet been opened to the kingdom of God. Jesus said to him:

> "The wind bloweth where it listeth, and thou hearest the sound thereof, but canst not tell whence it cometh, and whither it goeth: so is every one that is born of the Spirit." John 3:8

We cannot trace where the wind comes from and where it goes, and it is the same when a person is born of the Holy Spirit. "That which is born of the flesh is flesh." That which is born of the flesh is visible. We have been born in the flesh, so we have bodies that are visible and tangible.

When a person is born of the Holy Spirit, however, it is just like when the wind blows and we do not know where it has come from or where it is going. We do not know how we are born again. That is not to say that the individual is not aware himself that he is born again, but it takes place in the spirit of the individual and is not a visible phenomenon.

How Can These Things Be?

> "Nicodemus answered and said unto him, How can these things be?" John 3:9

How can these things be? When Nicodemus heard that he had to be born again, he became concerned and asked Jesus, "Are you saying that a man must enter into his mother's womb a second time and be born all over again?" Jesus explained that being born again is not a physical experience but a spiritual one.

> "Jesus answered and said unto him, Art thou a master of Israel, and knowest not these things?" John 3:10

The teachers of Israel should have understood all these things. The Jews had a highly developed system of worshiping and offering sacrifices to God, based on the five books of Moses. As they carefully observed all these ceremonies, they cleansed themselves of their sins once a year. Even in the Old Testament there are frequent references to the Holy Spirit, but it seems that Nicodemus was completely unaware of the significance of these important passages.

So this teacher of Israel asked, "How can these things be?" and Jesus said, "Art thou a master of Israel, and knowest not these things?" Let's turn to the book of Ezekiel and see how these things can be.

> "Then will I sprinkle clean water upon you, and ye shall be clean: from all your filthiness, and from all your idols, will I cleanse you. A new heart also will I give you, and a new spirit will I put within you: and I will take away the stony heart out of your flesh, and I will give you an heart of flesh."   Ezekiel 36:25-26

What did God say that He would give to man? He said, "A new spirit will I put within you." He announced in advance that He would put a new spirit, the Spirit of God, within the hearts of men. The prophets preached this message, and those who had studied the Old Testament scriptures had heard and knew it. It seems that Nicodemus, however, had completely forgotten about this new spirit. Jesus was explaining to Nicodemus about the workings of this spirit.

We Speak That We Do Know

> "Verily, verily, I say unto thee, We speak that we do know, and testify that we have seen; and ye receive not our witness."   John 3:11

Let's think about these words for a moment.

"Verily, verily, I say unto thee, We speak that we do know." Some people say that "we" in this verse refers to Jesus and His disciples, or Jesus and John the Baptist, but if you look at this passage in context, you can see that there was no one else there at the time. Who was Jesus referring to when He said, "we" here? He was including Himself in the trinity of God the Father, God the Son, and God the Holy Spirit.

In verse 11 where Jesus says, "ye," He was referring to the Pharisees. He had come to the society of the Pharisees and taught them, but they did not receive His witness. In John chapter 8, Jesus said:

"Ye shall seek me, and shall die in your sins." John 8:21

People asked Jesus, "Who on earth are You?" and Jesus answered:

"Even the same that I said unto you from the beginning." John 8: 25

When exactly was "the beginning"? In the Old Testament we read how God said to Abraham in Ur of the Chaldees, "Get thee out of thy country, and from thy kindred, and from thy father's house, unto a land that I will shew thee" Genesis 12:1, and Abraham obeyed and set out on his journey. At that time, the whole of the nation of Israel was already in Abraham's loins, since they are all the seed of Abraham. The God who spoke to Abraham continued to instruct the Israelites through the Old Testament scriptures. What is this God like? He is God the Father, God the Son, and God the Holy Spirit. So it was that when Jesus came into the world He said that He was: "Even the same that I said unto you from the beginning."

"We speak that we do know, and testify that we have seen." John 3:11

"We speak that we do know." God knows everything. From His throne on high, He looks down and knows everything that is going

41

on down here below, but that is not all that is meant here. Even while the Old Testament was being prepared, and the words that God spoke through the prophets were being written down, God could already see all the events of the future. When Jesus came into the world, He knew everything that was going to happen. This is what He meant when He said, "We speak that we do know."

Jesus was alone as He spoke to Nicodemus here, so why did He use the word, "we"? Nicodemus saw Jesus simply as one Man, but when Jesus used the plural pronoun, "we," He was revealing that He was God.

The One Who Has Ascended Into Heaven

"And ye receive not our witness." John 3:11

What is included in this "witness"? Jesus said:

"If I have told you earthly things, and ye believe not, how shall ye believe, if I tell you of heavenly things?" John 3:12

They did not even believe when Jesus spoke of earthly things, so how would they be able to believe if He spoke of heavenly things? They had the words of the Scriptures that God had given to them—the words that had been passed down to them through the prophets—and they had heard the parables Jesus had told them, but still they did not believe. How then would they believe if He spoke to them about heavenly things? To what can we compare the message Jesus gave Nicodemus regarding the path to the kingdom of God?

Perhaps a rather mundane example will serve to explain. When I was in the United States some years ago, I noticed that the person driving me around always used a map to find his way. He had a map of the area, and it not only covered the main roads, but all the side streets as well. Wherever we went, he consulted the map. A map is a kind of guide. It tells us how to arrive at our destination.

As believers, we are on our way to the kingdom of God and our guide is the Holy Bible. Even though Jesus taught these people the way to the kingdom of God, they failed to understand Him.

> "And no man hath ascended up to heaven, but he that came down from heaven, even the Son of man which is in heaven." John 3:13

Who is the One who came down from heaven? It is Jesus. And no one except Jesus has ascended into heaven. He was also in heaven at the time of the creation. In Proverbs chapter 8 it says:

> "Then I was by him, as one brought up with him: and I was daily his delight, rejoicing always before him." Proverbs 8:30

> The love of God is greater far
> Than tongue or pen can ever tell,
> It goes beyond the highest star,
> And reaches to the lowest hell
> The guilty pair, bowed down with care
> God gave His Son to win
> His erring child He reconciled
> And pardoned from His sin.
>
> Oh love of God, how rich and pure!
> How measureless and strong!
> It shall forevermore endure
> The saints' and angels' song.[11]

God's Son came down from heaven, such a far away place! He came from a distance beyond our imagination, and yet the Bible says:

> "Do not I fill heaven and earth? saith the Lord." Jeremiah 23:24

As we read in this verse, God fills the whole of the heaven and the earth. Let's turn now to Proverbs chapter 30. These verses are full of humility.

> "Surely I am more brutish than any man, and have not the understanding of a man. I neither learned wisdom, nor have the knowledge of the holy. Who hath ascended up into heaven, or descended? who hath gathered the wind in his fists? who hath bound the waters in a garment? who hath established all the ends of the earth? what is his name, and what is his son's name, if thou canst tell?"
>
> Proverbs 30:2-4

More than 700 years before Jesus came to the earth, the writer of the Proverbs asked, "What is his son's name?" No one knew at that time, but later an angel appeared to Mary and said, "And [you] shall bring forth a son, and they shall call his name Emmanuel" Matthew 1:23. Two thousand years have passed since then, and now we know what that Son's name is. There is a hymn that says:

> A little child may know
> Our Father's name of love;
> 'Tis written on the earth below,
> And on the sky above.[12]

This is a hymn that children often sing. We know the name of Jesus, but this great name, the name of the Son of God, is not a name that is known to just anyone.

Even So Must the Son of Man Be Lifted Up

> "And as Moses lifted up the serpent in the wilderness, even so must the Son of man be lifted up: That whosoever believeth in him should not perish, but have eternal life."
>
> John 3:14-15

Except a Man Be Born Again

Moses lifted up the serpent in the wilderness. Man seems to share a close relationship with the serpent, whether he likes it or not. What was it that caused man to sin? It was the serpent, wasn't it? In Genesis chapter 3, we have the words that God spoke to the serpent:

> "And I will put enmity between thee and the woman, and between thy seed and her seed; it shall bruise thy head, and thou shalt bruise his heel." Genesis 3:15

God's plan was accomplished when Jesus was lifted up and nailed to the cross. Jesus was lifted up in the air to hang on the cross.

> "Then said Jesus unto them, When ye have lifted up the Son of man, then shall ye know that I am he, and that I do nothing of myself; but as my Father hath taught me, I speak these things." John 8:28

Here, too, Jesus was speaking about His crucifixion. He referred to Himself as the "Son of man," since He had come into the world in the flesh. He said, "When ye have lifted up the Son of man, then shall ye know that I am he." In other words, they would come to understand after He had been crucified.

> "And I, if I be lifted up from the earth, will draw all men unto me. This he said, signifying what death he should die." John 12:32-33

What does it mean that Jesus would be lifted up from the earth? God spoke continually through the prophets in the Old Testament, telling of the crucifixion of Jesus. When the Israelites had come out of Egypt under the leadership of Moses, they began to complain against God and against Moses, and so God sent fiery serpents among them. These were poisonous snakes, and the Israelites who had been bitten by them were close to death. So Moses prayed to God, making an earnest plea for help, and God told him to make a bronze serpent and set it up on a pole.[13]

Let's try to imagine this situation. When Moses told the people to look at the serpent, innocent children would have raised their heads and looked up right away. Those who trusted more in their intellect and powers of reason, however, would have found this solution completely illogical and refused to look up. If they had been told to melt down the bronze serpent, break it into pieces with a hammer or grind it into powder to make a tonic that would heal them, they might have tried it, even though it would have involved a great effort on their part. But would they have found it easy to believe that they could be healed just by looking? Jesus also said something similar:

> "I thank thee, O Father, Lord of heaven and earth, because thou hast hid these things from the wise and prudent, and hast revealed them unto babes."
>
> Matthew 11:25

The Israelites were told simply to look at the bronze serpent. All they had to do was look. In our case, too, all we need to do is look to the cross, and yet there are so many pitiable people who will end up in hell because they continually discuss the cross from every possible angle instead of just looking at it.

The Israelites who had been bitten were told to look and they looked. They did not question or try to rationalize what was happening, they simply looked and they were healed.

> "And the Lord said unto Moses, Make thee a fiery serpent, and set it upon a pole: and it shall come to pass, that every one that is bitten, when he looketh upon it, shall live. And Moses made a serpent of brass, and put it upon a pole, and it came to pass, that if a serpent had bitten any man, when he beheld the serpent of brass, he lived."
>
> Numbers 21:8-9

Doesn't this sound like a dream? When it says "look" here, is it used in the ordinary sense of the word? Just as Moses lifted up the serpent on a pole in the wilderness, Jesus, too, was lifted up and nailed to the cross. When Jesus was nailed to the cross, it was not merely a case of the death penalty being carried out; He was crucified in accordance with the words that had been recorded in the Scriptures. It was as the Bible says, "The Son of man goeth as it is written of him" Matthew 26:24.[14]

Let's go back to John chapter 3.

> "And no man hath ascended up to heaven, but he that came down from heaven, even the Son of man which is in heaven. And as Moses lifted up the serpent in the wilderness, even so must the Son of man be lifted up: That whosoever believeth in him should not perish, but have eternal life." John 3:13-15

When Moses lifted up the serpent in the wilderness, the snakebites of all the people who looked at it were healed. "Even so must the Son of man be lifted up: That whosoever believeth in him should not perish, but have eternal life." God's aim in giving us His word was not so that we might lead religious lives of reading the Bible and singing hymns without being able to go to the kingdom of God. He gave us His word in order that we might receive eternal life.

Being born again itself is a matter of becoming connected to eternal life. The path that had been cut off between man and God has been reconnected. The path that Jesus took, being lifted up and nailed to the cross is the path to the kingdom of God. Jesus was explaining the moment when we come into contact with this eternal life.

Nicodemus probably heard the voice of God in his heart on that day and was deeply moved. The path to the kingdom of God is opened only through Jesus Christ, but that path is a narrow one. Many people make all kinds of efforts in their attempts to prepare themselves to be able to go to the kingdom of God, but there is no need to make such efforts or to do anything at all. Just as the Israelites were healed simply by looking at the serpent, we become born again simply by looking to Jesus. Once a person has had this experience, he finds that the Bible also explains the path he is to take as he lives his life as a child of God.

9

For God So Loved The World

John 3:16-21

When the Bible says, "For God so loved the world,"
how far does this "so" extend?
God loved the world so much that He handed over to the world
His beloved only begotten Son, so that we might come to believe
without any effort on our own part.
He made it so that all we need to do is
believe that the suffering on the cross was for our sins, for my sins.

John 3:16-21

[16]For God so loved the world, that he gave his only begotten Son, that whosoever believeth in him should not perish, but have everlasting life. [17]For God sent not his Son into the world to condemn the world; but that the world through him might be saved. [18]He that believeth on him is not condemned: but he that believeth not is condemned already, because he hath not believed in the name of the only begotten Son of God. [19]And this is the condemnation, that light is come into the world, and men loved darkness rather than light, because their deeds were evil. [20]For every one that doeth evil hateth the light, neither cometh to the light, lest his deeds should be reproved. [21]But he that doeth truth cometh to the light, that his deeds may be made manifest, that they are wrought in God.

Whosoever Believeth in Him

John chapter 3 verse 16 is probably the most well-known verse in the whole Bible. Even people who do not go to church or do not believe in Jesus will, most likely, be familiar at least with this verse. As a child, I even learned this verse as a song.

> "For God so loved the world, that he gave his only begotten Son, that whosoever believeth in him should not perish, but have everlasting life."
> John 3:16

In this verse it says, "whosoever believeth in him." The New International Version of the Bible uses the word "everyone" here, while in the Living Bible the translators preferred "anyone." Whether it says "whoever," "everyone," or "anyone," it includes every single person in the world.

I am really not sure how to give full expression to this verse, but I will do my best. It says, "For God so loved the world." What does "so" mean here? When I was a child, someone had set these words to music, and we used to sing them. Even though I sang along, I did not know what the words meant, and I did not, of course, know what this "so" meant either. As I attended church and read the Bible, I learned that God sent His only begotten Son into the world and that this Son was crucified and died. It was a long time, however, before I came to a firm belief in this truth.

Some people may come to believe in an instant without going through a long process as I did. The criminal who hung on the cross next to Jesus, for example, had lived as he pleased all his life in this world and then, just moments before he died, he came to believe. Did he have time to attend church? He did not have time to do any good deeds and neither did he have any way of demonstrating his faith through his actions. He was under the sentence of death and his hands and feet were nailed to the cross, so he could not do anything.

We do not know how rich this man was, but he was not able to give everything he had to the poor. Neither was there any need for him to resolve to be good if only he could be released from his present plight. He was about to breathe his last but as he hung there on the cross, he came to believe in Jesus. It did not take any effort on his own part.

If we read the Bible carefully, we find that it contains a message that goes beyond anything that we could possibly imagine. The gospel is recorded very simply and plainly and yet many people are not able to go to the kingdom of God because their own thoughts get in the way. There are people who have a hard time getting to the kingdom of God because they think it is difficult. That is not to say that it actually is difficult to go to the kingdom of God, but they think it is difficult and this prevents them from going. If it were difficult to enter the kingdom of God, all we would have to do is work hard at it. But since it is so simple, people tend to look for it in all the wrong places.

Let's take an example from geometry. A right angle is 90°. If you draw a right angle that is just one degree out, or even one tenth of a degree out, as you extend the lines of the angle, the error will become very noticeable.

The same is true of the gospel. Since it is so simple and easy, people ask, "Isn't there something more for me to do?" and they try to find something to add to it. They give themselves a hard time, creating heavy burdens for themselves.

There is a story about a taxi driver who had an especially good day and earned a lot more than he had expected. He was in a very good mood and as he drove along, he decided to give a free ride to the next person who got into his taxi whoever it might be. He saw an elderly lady walking along, groaning under the weight of the heavy bundle she was carrying on her head. So the taxi driver called out to her:

"Hop in, and I'll give you a ride."

"Oh my! This is very nice of you, young man," the elderly lady said as she got into the taxi.

The taxi driver drove along for a while, whistling as he went, but then he heard the sound of groaning coming from the back seat. He looked behind him only to find the elderly lady still balancing her bundle on her head.

"Why don't you put your bundle down on the seat beside you?" he asked her.

"Oh no, I couldn't do that! It's enough that you are giving me a ride. I can't expect you to take my bags as well!"

There are many such people amongst those who believe in Jesus. They think, "It's enough that God has saved me. How could I shamelessly unload the burden of my sins upon Him as well?"

Because It Is So Easy

There are very many religious people in this world who are still carrying the burden of their sin. What did Jesus say to such people?

"Come unto me, all ye that labour and are heavy laden, and I will give you rest." Matthew 11:28

"And ye shall know the truth, and the truth shall make you free." John 8:32

"If the Son therefore shall make you free, ye shall be free indeed." John 8:36

Jesus said, "Except a man be born again, he cannot see the kingdom of God" John 3:3. When the Bible says, "For God so loved the world," how far does this "so" extend? God loved the world so much that He handed over to the world His beloved only begotten Son, so that we might come to believe without any effort on our own part. He made it so that all we need to do is believe that the suffering on the cross was for our sins, for my sins. He made it so easy for us to believe, but there are many people who are not able to enter the kingdom of God precisely because it is so easy. The very thought of this sends my head swimming.

> "Many will say to me in that day, Lord, Lord, have we not prophesied in thy name? and in thy name have cast out devils? and in thy name done many wonderful works? And then will I profess unto them, I never knew you: depart from me, ye that work iniquity."
>
> Matthew 7:22-23

Countless people build up their store of good deeds and enthusiasm, but in the end, God will tell them to depart from Him and drive them far away. Why do you think this is? These people will have missed one important fact, one very simple truth.

As a child is being born into this world, does he do anything at all for his parents to help them out in the process? Does the child do anything to enable himself to be born? Are the child's services or strength needed? Nothing at all is required of the child. The only strength that is needed is that of the mother. The child can do nothing. He may kick around a bit while he is in the womb, but he does not have the strength to help in the course of his own birth.

What does all this show us? God established these laws to govern the process of human birth. It is the same when it comes to being born as children of God; the Bible tells us that this is not possible through man's own strength.

> "If thou be righteous, what givest thou him? or what receiveth he of thine hand? Thy wickedness may hurt a man as thou art; and thy righteousness may profit the son of man." Job 35:7-8

> "All our righteousnesses are as filthy rags." Isaiah 64:6

Our own righteousness is like old rags. No matter how good we may be in human terms, we cannot attain God's standards. Such goodness is only necessary within human society; it has nothing to do with being born into the kingdom of God. Neither human effort nor human strength is needed when an individual is born as a son of God.

Look Unto Me

> "For God so loved the world, that he gave his only begotten Son, that whosoever believeth in him should not perish, but have everlasting life." John 3:16

John chapter 1 verse 9 expresses this in a slightly different way:

> "That was the true Light, which lighteth every man that cometh into the world."

The Son of God came into the world of man. Also, this light shines on each one of us individually. "The true Light, which lighteth every man that cometh into the world," is given to us on an individual basis.

> There's a light in the valley of death now for me,
> Since Jesus came into my heart.[1]

Let's think about this light. People inclined toward mysticism may decide that it is necessary to see a physical light since the apostle Paul saw a light. So they go to pray in the mountains or in some kind of prayer house. They close their eyes tight and cry out, "Lord, Lord!" and they see a sudden flash of light. Then they get excited and take this as being an answer to their prayers. The light they have seen, however, could well have been from the headlights of a car passing along the mountain road, or perhaps a firefly shimmering near their closed eyes. That is not the kind of light that is referred to here in John's Gospel. No light, no matter how bright, is of any use to our spirits without Jesus. The true light is the light of the knowledge of Jesus Christ, the light in the heart of a person who discovers Christ.

When we studied John chapter 3 verse 14, we read in the book of Numbers that, when the Israelites were in the wilderness, some fiery serpents came out and bit those who had spoken against God and against Moses. At that time, what did God tell Moses to do?

> "Make thee a fiery serpent, and set it upon a pole: and it shall come to pass, that every one that is bitten, when he looketh upon it, shall live." Numbers 21:8

Looking up at the bronze serpent was the only way for them to be healed. Believing also has to be this easy. It is so simple, however, that some people have a hard time with it. If we were to analyze this cure based on our knowledge of chemistry, taking into consideration how the poison from the snake enters the body and causes the proteins in the body to coagulate, it would be difficult to believe in a cure that simply involved looking at a bronze serpent. So it is that a person may perish by depending on his own limited store of knowledge.

In the book of Isaiah there is a verse that says, "Look unto me, and be ye saved, all the ends of the earth" Isaiah 45:22. It says, "Look unto me."

There is a story about a young man in England who was trying to make his way to church through a snowstorm one winter's morning. It was snowing so heavily that the road was blocked and he could not get to his usual church, so he called in at a little church that he happened to pass on the way. There were less than twenty people gathered there and their pastor had not arrived yet. In his place in the pulpit stood a shabby man who looked like he might have been a tailor. He was reading from the book of Isaiah. "Look unto me, and be ye saved." Isaiah 45:22 And then he kept shouting, "Look unto me." His pronunciation was not even quite correct and yet he repeated these words again and again:

"The Bible says, 'Look unto me.' It does not hurt to look. You only have to look. Anyone can look. Look unto Me! I hung on the cross. Look unto Me! I'm shedding drops of blood."

The speaker put everything he had into his sermon. The young man wondered what in the world this preacher was talking about. "He may be uneducated," he thought, "but how many more times is he going to repeat those words, 'Look unto me'?"

Then, suddenly, the preacher caught the young man's eye and shouted:

"Why are you looking at me? Look to Jesus! Look right now to Jesus who died for you!"

The young man was startled as he realized:

"Oh! That's right! Jesus died for me!"

At that moment, he came to believe. Later, that young man put his whole life into spreading the gospel and became a great evangelist. His name was Charles Spurgeon.[2] Perhaps you have heard of him.

Which He Had Promised Afore in the Holy Scriptures Concerning His Son

There is a hymn that includes the lines:

> Son of Man, exalted High!
> Let Him in! Let Him in![3]

It says that Jesus was exalted high, and we should let Him in.

"God, who at sundry times and in divers manners spake in time past unto the fathers by the prophets, Hath in these last days spoken unto us by his Son." Hebrews 1:1-2

A continuous stream of prophets wrote about Jesus.

"Of which salvation the prophets have enquired and searched diligently, who prophesied of the grace that should come unto you: Searching what, or what manner of time the Spirit of Christ which was in them did signify, when it testified beforehand the sufferings of Christ, and the glory that should follow." 1 Peter 1:10-11

All of this had already been recorded in the Old Testament.

The Spirit of God moved the hearts of the prophets to write down all that He told them, but even as they wrote, they did not know what it all meant. David, for example, wrote:

"My God, my God, why hast thou forsaken me?" Psalm 22:1

"For dogs have compassed me: the assembly of the wicked have inclosed me: they pierced my hands and my feet." Psalm 22:16

"They part my garments among them, and cast lots upon my vesture." Psalm 22:18

David had already written all of this down one thousand years before the time of Jesus. One day, Jesus was breaking bread with His twelve disciples and as He gave a morsel to Judas He said to him, "That thou doest, do quickly" John 13:27. Then He also said:

> "The Son of man indeed goeth, as it is written of him: but woe to that man by whom the Son of man is betrayed! good were it for that man if he had never been born." Mark 14:21

Jesus said that He was going to go the way that had been determined for Him. "I will die as it has been recorded in the Old Testament scriptures, but it would have been better for that man if he had never been born." This was because the wrath of God would extend to him. Judas ate with them and then went out. He was in charge of the moneybox, so the other disciples would have thought he had gone to buy something. But Judas had gone to sell Jesus to the chief priests. The price for this sale, thirty shekels of silver,[4] had already been recorded in the Old Testament.

> "And I said unto them, If ye think good, give me my price; and if not, forbear. So they weighed for my price thirty pieces of silver. And the Lord said unto me, Cast it unto the potter: a goodly price that I was prised at of them. And I took the thirty pieces of silver, and cast them to the potter in the house of the Lord." Zechariah 11:12-13

One of Jesus' disciples betrayed Him for thirty shekels of silver. Already in Genesis chapter 3 we have a record of a prophecy about the death of Jesus. God said to the serpent that he would bruise the heel of the seed of the woman. Also Jesus Himself said, "And I, if I be lifted up from the earth, will draw all men unto me" John 12:32, and He was indeed lifted up and nailed to the cross. Judas Iscariot helped in this matter. So the Bible also foretold the way in which Jesus would die.

> "The gospel of God, (Which he had promised afore by his prophets in the holy scriptures,) Concerning his Son."
>
> Romans 1:1-3

When it says, "the holy scriptures," here, it means the Old Testament. The promise that God made in advance through the Old Testament prophets about Jesus Christ, the only begotten Son of God, is the gospel.

> "Now to him that is of power to stablish you according to my gospel, and the preaching of Jesus Christ, according to the revelation of the mystery, which was kept secret since the world began, But now is made manifest, and by the scriptures of the prophets, according to the commandment of the everlasting God, made known to all nations for the obedience of faith: To God only wise, be glory through Jesus Christ for ever. Amen." Romans 16:25-27

It says here that this gospel has been "made known to all nations for obedience of faith;" not just to one particular nation. The gospel is there for everyone, for "whosoever believeth."

Wretched Man that I Am

As I read the Bible, I often consider the difference between the thoughts of man and the thoughts of God. The Bible says, "For my thoughts are not your thoughts, neither are your ways my ways, saith the Lord" Isaiah 55:8. Sometimes, when I see really evil characters, people who commit heinous crimes, I marvel that Jesus died even for the likes of them.

Then there are those who use their writings to lure others into a clever trap, forcing them into a corner from which there is no escape. This is more frightening than the threat of a nasty punch or some other physical injury. Such people appear to be quite respectable on the outside and yet they torment others, pinning them to the wall. No matter how carefully you may look, you will not be able to see physically the evil within man even through the lens of a microscope. Even as people smile and shake hands, their hearts are full of evil intent. This evil is invisible, but it moves into action whenever the necessity arises. It is really quite strange, isn't it?

David was a good king as well as a prophet, and yet there was still one occasion on which he committed a terrible sin. One day as he was looking down his palace, he saw a beautiful woman bathing and he summoned her. Since he was king, he could do as he pleased. Later, to hide his sin, he summoned the woman's husband, Uriah, from the battlefield. Uriah came, battle-worn and covered with dust. Such was his faithfulness to his king, however, that he did not return home, but slept at the door of the royal palace with all the other servants of the king. David panicked and tried to push Uriah to go home. Why did David behave like this? He had slept with this man's wife and she had conceived. In the end, since Uriah slept at the king's palace, refusing to go home, David sent him to the front line of the battle so that he would be killed.

Later David realized that he had committed a terrible sin and he wept bitterly. Psalm 51 contains David's words of repentance.

> "Create in me a clean heart, O God; and renew a right spirit within me."
> Psalm 51:10

David's life reveals both the good and evil aspects of human nature. Once when I turned on the television, I happened to see a movie in which the hero was a really wicked man. He took a machine gun and shot at some people and they all fell to the ground. He just mowed them down. "He's good with that gun," I thought. Later in the movie, when the police began to chase this man, however, I found myself hoping that he would not get caught. I do not know where this attitude came from. It is true that the movie would come to an end if the villain was caught, but quite apart from that, I simply wanted him to survive to the end.

When I find myself reacting like that, I can see that there is evil inside of me as well. The apostle Paul was also aware of this evil that co-existed inside of him as he said, "O wretched man that I am!" Romans 7:24. We all have this sinful nature inside of us, so are we in a position to be able to condemn Judas Iscariot for betraying Jesus as though Judas were the only person who had any evil inside him? After Judas betrayed Jesus, his conscience tormented him so much that he took the money he had received and threw it down in the temple. Then he went away and committed suicide by hanging himself.

When the Bible says, "that whosoever believeth," this "whosoever" applies to everyone—all the different kinds of people that exist, including those you hate and those who hate you. Everyone is included.

> "For God so loved the world, that he gave his only begotten Son, that whosoever believeth in him should not perish, but have everlasting life." John 3:16

When people begin to feel uncertain about their lives on this earth, they tend to think impulsively about life after death, imagining how peaceful everything will be then. They have an image of heaven that stems from their human desires, but such is not eternal life. People think they will go to heaven after they die. They live for seventy, eighty, or maybe even one hundred years, but the image of heaven that they conjure up during that time, using all the powers of imagination that they have within them, will be nothing like eternal life on the level that it actually is. Eternal life cannot be measured in terms of a world of blessings and pleasures where the spirits of men go when their life in the flesh comes to an end.

Eternal life is nothing like that; it is given by the Spirit of God who created the heaven and the earth and it is given to everyone who believes. The Holy Spirit is eternal life and this eternal life must enter the hearts of men.

For God So Loved the World

"For God so loved the world, that he gave his only begotten Son."

How did God give His only begotten Son? How did God love the world?

In observance of their law, the Jews continued to shed the blood of an animal each time they offered a sacrifice to God. Jesus, however, fulfilled the whole of the law as He offered His own body as the eternal sacrificial offering.

> "But this man, because he continueth ever, hath an unchangeable priesthood. Wherefore he is able also to save them to the uttermost that come unto God by him, seeing he ever liveth to make intercession for them." Hebrews 7:24-25

It says here that "he ever liveth." Even now, Jesus is at the right hand of God, making intercession for our sin. We can always confess before the Lord the sins that stain our lives from day to day, and God has promised us through the Holy Spirit that this is all we need to do. The Jews offered sacrifices continually, changing their priests time and again, but now Jesus, the eternal High Priest, has dealt with our sins by offering Himself once for all. All we have to do is believe this fact.

> "Nor yet that he should offer himself often, as the high priest entereth into the holy place every year with blood of others; For then must he often have suffered since the foundation of the world: but now once in the end of the world hath he appeared to put away sin by the sacrifice of himself." Hebrews 9:25-26

If the sacrifice of Jesus had been like that offered annually by the high priests, He would have had to die often, but this was not the case. In the Bible it says that He appeared "in these last days" Hebrews 1:2 as God foretold in the prophets, or as it says in the verse above, "in the end of the world." What is meant by "these last days" or "the end of the world"? It is the time when Jesus appeared.

Let's consider this matter in terms of BC and AD. For us living at the present time, "the end of the world" lies in the past. People who lived during the period of history before Christ believed in the Messiah who was to come, but we who live in the Christian era, AD, believe in what the Messiah accomplished when He came. So people who lived before Jesus came into the world looked to the future and believed, while we, today, look back and believe in Christ who died in the past.

> "So Christ was once offered to bear the sins of many; and unto them that look for him shall he appear the second time without sin unto salvation." Hebrews 9:28

Did Jesus offer His body gradually over a long period of time, or did He offer Himself once for all? There is a verse in the Old Testament that says, "I will remove the iniquity of that land in one day" Zechariah 3:9. How many days did it take for sin to enter this world? It did not even take one day; sin entered in just a moment in time, the moment when Adam ate from the fruit of the tree of the knowledge of good and evil. In that case, how long would it take for sin to be forgiven? When Jesus was crucified, did He say, "It is taking two or three days to finish it"? No. On that day, He took upon Himself the sin of all mankind and said, "It is finished" John 19:30.

The Bible says, "So Christ was once offered to bear the sins of many; and unto them that look for him shall he appear the second time without sin unto salvation." This is a promise that Jesus will come again later to completely transform our bodies.

> "By the which will we are sanctified through the offering of the body of Jesus Christ once for all." Hebrews 10:10

> All sin forgiven, I stand in Him here,
> One of His people eternally dear!
> ...
> Life has no menace and death has no fear![5]

"All sin forgiven." If I had been forgiven and sanctified through my own efforts, I would not be able to sing this hymn. If we claimed carelessly that we have been forgiven or sanctified, or that we are holy, it would sound arrogant, wouldn't it? But God has sanctified us so we sing these words out of gratitude.

> "But this man, after he had offered one sacrifice for sins for ever, sat down on the right hand of God." Hebrews 10:12

Did Christ offer a sacrifice for the sins we committed in the past, or did He offer one sacrifice for sins for all time?

> Oh love of God, how rich and pure!
> ...
> It shall forever more endure,
> The saints' and angels' song.[6]

What kind of love is this that endures forever? It is not the kind of love that gives salvation and then takes it away again if we do not listen to what we are told. It is an eternal, unchanging love.

> Nothing but the blood of Jesus:
> All my praise for this I bring.[7]

Our sins have been forgiven through the blood that Jesus shed on the cross, but how far does that forgiveness go? It is eternal, but where does eternity begin and where does it end? One believer in the past expressed eternity by saying that he would live eternally where the healing waters flow.

He Gave His Only Begotten Son

> "For by one offering he hath perfected for ever them that are sanctified. Whereof the Holy Ghost also is a witness to us: for after that he had said before, This is the covenant that I will make with them after those days, saith the Lord, I will put my laws into their hearts, and in their minds will I write them; And their sins and iniquities will I remember no more. Now where remission of these is, there is no more offering for sin." Hebrews 10:14-18

Here it says, "For by one offering..." Who is this holy offering? It is God's only begotten Son, His one and only Son. It would not have been so precious if God had had several sons and said to one of them, "I want you to go into the world and be crucified, but if you don't go, I'll send one of your brothers." But God gave us His only Son. "For by one offering he hath perfected for ever them that are sanctified."

"For God so loved the world, that he gave his only begotten Son."

How do you think God must have felt as He gave the only Son He had? This brings to mind the time when Abraham took his son, Isaac, to Mount Moriah. Abraham set out on a journey in order to offer Isaac as a sacrifice in obedience to God's command, a command that he had to obey. Abraham had not been young and vigorous when this son was born to him; Isaac was born when

Abraham was old and his wife was already past the age of childbearing. She would have given up all hope of ever having any children, so they must have doted on this son as they were bringing him up. How must Abraham have felt when God commanded him to offer his only son as sacrifice?

As they were on their way to Mount Moriah, Isaac said to his father:

> "Behold the fire and the wood: but where is the lamb for a burnt offering?"
> Genesis 22:7

Abraham could not bring himself to tell his son the truth, so he said:

> "My son, God will provide himself a lamb for a burnt offering."
> Genesis 22:8

The son simply followed his father. When they arrived at Mount Moriah, Abraham bound his son tightly on the altar. Then he took out his knife, but just as he was about to kill his son, God stopped him. It was clear that Abraham had already offered his son in his heart, and Isaac was given his life again.

In the same way, God's only Son suffered atrocious agony and death for the sake of mankind, but it was God's plan to bring His Son back to life again. He had to be brought back to life because only then would we be able to live.

> "Verily, verily, I say unto you, Except a corn of wheat fall into the ground and die, it abideth alone: but if it die, it bringeth forth much fruit."
> John 12:24

Only through the death of Jesus—the "corn of wheat"—could the spirits of many be saved.

That They Might Have Eternal Life

"For God so loved the world, that he gave his only begotten Son, that whosoever believeth in him should not perish, but have everlasting life." John 3:16

What sort of life is this eternal life? Long ago the prophet Daniel was taken captive to Babylon where he was made an official of that country. One day while he was living there, he received a command from God.

"But go thou thy way till the end be: for thou shalt rest, and stand in thy lot at the end of the days." Daniel 12:13

These words indicate that some day the eternal promise would be fulfilled. Daniel died in hope because of this promise that he had received from God.

"And at that time shall Michael stand up, the great prince which standeth for the children of thy people: and there shall be a time of trouble, such as never was since there was a nation even to that same time: and at that time thy people shall be delivered, every one that shall be found written in the book. And many of them that sleep in the dust of the earth shall awake, some to everlasting life, and some to shame and everlasting contempt." Daniel 12:1-2

God promised the many people of Old Testament times who followed His will that He would give them eternal life when this world came to an end.

Then, when Jesus came to this world, He also promised eternal life, but on a different level, to those who listened to His words.

Let's think again here about John chapter 3 verse 16. When it says, "That whosoever believeth in him should not perish, but have everlasting life," it means that God has forgiven us, sinners that we are.

> I was once a sinner, but I came
> Pardon to receive from my Lord:
> This was freely given, and I found
> That He always kept His word.
>
> There's a new name written down in glory,
> And it's mine, O yes, it's mine![8]

As this hymn says, we have been pardoned for our sins. We were once sinners but we have received eternal forgiveness. What promise has God given to us?

> "Verily, verily, I say unto you, He that heareth my word, and believeth on him that sent me, hath everlasting life, and shall not come into condemnation; but is passed from death unto life. Verily, verily, I say unto you, The hour is coming, and now is, when the dead shall hear the voice of the Son of God: and they that hear shall live."
>
> John 5:24-25

How can the dead hear the voice of the Son of God? Common sense tells us that the nerves of the dead decompose, including the nerves of the ear, and there is no way that the dead can hear. But let's think about the words that God spoke to Adam.

> "But of the tree of the knowledge of good and evil, thou shalt not eat of it: for in the day that thou eatest thereof thou shalt surely die."
>
> Genesis 2:17

This death meant a break off in communication between Adam and God. Even after Adam ate from the fruit of the tree of the knowledge of good and evil, he lived for a very long time. But what happened to his eyes? They became opened to the world, and he came to know that he too belonged to the world. Before this happened, he belonged to paradise. Adam and Eve were naked as they lived in the Garden of Eden, but they were not embarrassed or ashamed. This was no problem in paradise. As soon as they ate the forbidden fruit, however, their eyes were opened. They became aware that someone was looking at them and they became aware of themselves. On that day, man died to God. It is to man in this state that God has given the Bible.

I Give Eternal Life

Why did the Jews read the Old Testament and keep its words close to their hearts for such a long time?

> "Search the scriptures; for in them ye think ye have eternal life: and they are they which testify of me." John 5:39

We read the Scriptures in order to receive eternal life. The Bible bears witness of Jesus, and we read it to come to know Jesus and, through Him, receive eternal life.

> "But these are written, that ye might believe that Jesus is the Christ, the Son of God; and that believing ye might have life through his name." John 20:31

John's Gospel, too, was recorded in order that we might believe that Jesus is the Christ and have eternal life. If we consider all 66 books of the Bible, few of them put as much emphasis on the matter of eternal life as John's Gospel does. Who is Jesus? He is the Son of God, the Christ or "anointed One," promised in the Old Testament. It is through faith in Him that we receive eternal life.

> "And this is life eternal, that they might know thee the only true God, and Jesus Christ, whom thou hast sent." John 17:3

This promise of eternal life is so very holy! If it were not for this promise, what hope would we have by which to live?

> "And I give unto them eternal life; and they shall never perish, neither shall any man pluck them out of my hand. My Father, which gave

them me, is greater than all; and no man is able to pluck them out of my Father's hand." John 10:28-29

No one can pluck us out of the Father's hand. Who can possibly do this? Not even the devil can snatch us out of His hand, since God is greater than all things and fills all things. No one can snatch us away, because even though Christians also must die somehow, somewhere, all those who have come to realize and believe that God loves them so much that He has forgiven all their sins will meet in the eternal heavenly kingdom, wherever that may be. It is not possible for any of them to be omitted, since they have eternal life. When we drift away from God, however, when we sin or do something for which we should be disciplined and do not confess what we have done, we feel pain in our hearts.

The Door that Leads to Life

"And this is the will of him that sent me, that every one which seeth the Son, and believeth on him, may have everlasting life: and I will raise him up at the last day." John 6:40

Even though Jesus promised that on the last day He would raise up all those who have eternal life, many people did not heed His words.

"Strive to enter in at the strait gate: for many, I say unto you, will seek to enter in, and shall not be able." Luke 13:24

"Enter ye in at the strait gate: for wide is the gate, and broad is the way, that leadeth to destruction, and many there be which go in thereat: Because strait is the gate, and narrow is the way, which leadeth unto life, and few there be that find it." Matthew 7:13-14

"Many will say to me in that day, Lord, Lord, have we not prophesied in thy name? and in thy name have cast out devils? and in thy name done many wonderful works? And then will I profess unto them, I never knew you: depart from me, ye that work iniquity."

Matthew 7:22-23

Many people will say that they did all kinds of work for God while living in this world, and yet God will say to them, "I never knew you," because they have rejected His will. A person must first receive eternal life and then he can walk with God.

The Holy Spirit brings us to realize that Jesus is our Savior and that He has forgiven our sins for all time. Since we have received God's love, when we have fellowship with other believers, we understand each other's hearts. When we hear someone else's testimony of salvation, we can identify with them, and hymns that were once meaningless to us now become our very own. Who makes all of this possible? It is the work of the Holy Spirit of God, and it is very important to ask yourself if you are part of this work. If not, you could be one of those who on the last day are addressed with the words, "I never knew you." Religious activities may be necessary in human society, but they are of no use at all when we stand before God.

He that Believeth on Me Hath Everlasting Life

"Verily, verily, I say unto you, He that believeth on me hath everlasting life."

John 6:47

Does it say in this verse that he who believes will have eternal life, or already has eternal life? Jesus, the Son of God, was born without sin to the virgin Mary and He was crucified and died for your sin and mine. God gave us Jesus as a gift so that He might forgive the sins of the whole world. If my sins are included and I myself am included, then I have been crucified with Christ.

"I am crucified with Christ: nevertheless I live; yet not I, but Christ liveth in me: and the life which I now live in the flesh I live by the faith of the Son of God, who loved me, and gave himself for me."

Galatians 2:20

When was I crucified with Christ? On the day that Adam sinned, we were already in his body, and God knew that we would be born as sinners. We were born in bodies just like that of Adam, so God promised that He would send His Son into the world for the sake of sinners such as we are. This promise is the Old Testament. Jesus came to this world as promised in the Old Testament and died to atone for Adam's sin in his place, so we too died with Him.

> Dying with Jesus, by death reckoned mine;[9]

If it were not for this principle, if I as an individual had not died with Jesus when He was crucified, everyone who sang this hymn would be deceiving himself.

We have received many blessings, or perhaps I should say we have met with blessings. This world is full of blessings. Every time you sneeze someone blesses you. Nevertheless, there are very many people who have yet to receive the true blessing, the blessing freely given to us by God's command. What is God's command?

His Commandment Is Life Everlasting

There is a hymn I used to sing parrot fashion when I was a young boy, completely oblivious to what it was all about.

> On us has fallen God's clear command:
> In this garden land let us go labor![10]

I memorized every word of this hymn.

But for a long time I lived my life ignorant of God's commandment. One day, however, as I was reading through John's Gospel, I came across these words of Jesus:

"And I know that his commandment is life everlasting." John 12:50

The Bible says that God's commandment is that we should receive eternal life. I was really elated when I realized that this eternal life has been given to me for free and nothing was expected of me in return. The Bible says, "Whosoever shall not receive the kingdom of God as a little child, he shall not enter therein" Mark 10:15. Receiving eternal life is really very simple.

"For I have not spoken of myself; but the Father which sent me, he gave me a commandment, what I should say, and what I should speak. And I know that his commandment is life everlasting: whatsoever I speak therefore, even as the Father said unto me, so I speak." John 12:49-50

Jesus did not make up the words He spoke to us; He received the commandments of God and passed them on to us. Did Jesus tell us to be diligent in keeping the law? Or did He command us to attend church regularly? It is not a question of belonging to a certain Christian denomination; all that matters is that we believe. The important point is that God's commandment is eternal life.

"For God so loved the world, that he gave his only begotten Son, that whosoever believeth in him should not perish, but have everlasting life." John 3:16

There is a world of difference between God having given something to us and our trying to give something to God. What can we possibly give to God? All that remains for us to do is simply place our faith in Jesus Christ, God's only begotten Son. We need only relax and put our trust in Him.

I still remember a story I read in a book some time ago. There was a mother who had lost her son, her only child. She used every penny she had in her attempt to find him. She put out announcements on the radio and advertisements in the newspapers, but it was all to no avail. When all her money had run out, she began to search for her son on foot. Then after several years like this, she was walking through a poverty-stricken neighborhood one day when she noticed a child who looked like her son. His face was filthy dirty, his clothes were in rags, and his skin had broken out in sores, but it was definitely her son. What would the boy's mother have said?

"My son! Do you know how long I've been looking for you? Come on, let's go home."

Suppose the son had then replied:

"Mom, I can't go home like this. I'm too dirty. Let me earn some money, take a bath, and get some new clothes, and then I'll come."

How would the mother have felt? Do these words indicate that the son knows what is in his mother's heart? If he had not grown up at all and was still only a very young child, he probably would have simply run to his mother's arms and wept for joy. Since he had grown up a little, however, he would be concerned about such irrelevant matters and probably say something like:

"Just look at me. Look at my situation!"

Is there any need for us to weigh up our circumstances when we turn to God? God is calling to us, telling us to come to Him, as the hymn says:

> Come home! Come home!
> You are weary at heart.[11]

In Luke's Gospel we find the parable of the prodigal son. There was a man who had two sons. One day the younger son approached his father and asked for his share of the family fortune. He then took what was given to him and left for a distant place where he lived a life of dissipation. When he had used up all his money in this way, he found a job looking after pigs. He was so hungry that he longed even to eat the pods that were given to the swine, but there was no one who would feed him. He would even have eaten the slightly rotten fruit from the pigs' swill, if he could have. So he began to think:

"In my father's house the hired men have more than enough to eat, but here I am dying of hunger. Wouldn't I be better off if I returned to my father and asked him to use me as one of his hired men? Then at least I would have plenty to eat."

So he set off for home. While he was still a long way off, his father saw him and came running to him. The father embraced his son and rejoiced, saying, "For this my son was dead, and is alive again."[12]

Then there is the story of a woman who had ten silver coins, but she lost one of them. She turned her house upside down as she searched carefully in every corner until she found it. Then she was so happy that she called together her friends and neighbors to celebrate with her.[13]

There is also the parable of a shepherd who had one hundred sheep and lost one of them. So he left behind the 99 sheep and went in search of the one that was lost. When he found it, he brought it home rejoicing and held a feast with his friends to celebrate.[14] As Jesus told this parable, He said, "Likewise joy shall be in heaven over one sinner that repenteth, more than over ninety and nine just persons, which need no repentance" Luke 15:7.

The common thread that runs through all of these parables is that people were searching. Did the younger son return to his father expecting to be taken back as a son? He was even prepared to work as a servant. But how did the father greet his son? He did not receive him as a servant but as the son he had lost. The father found his son, the woman found her silver coin, and who found the lost sheep? It was the shepherd. All power and authority lie in God's hands. We, too, were lost before God, but now we have been found again. It is not that we found God, but He found us.

The Son Did Not Come to Condemn the World

> "For God sent not his Son into the world to condemn the world; but that the world through him might be saved." John 3:17

From this verse we can see that God did not send His Son into the world in order to judge the world. The Son did not come to rebuke or condemn mankind. God's purpose in sending His Son into the world was in order that all the people in the world might be saved through Jesus.

> "He that believeth on him is not condemned: but he that believeth not is condemned already, because he hath not believed in the name of the only begotten Son of God." John 3:18

A person who believes is not condemned, but a person who does not believe has already been condemned. No one under God's condemnation can enter the kingdom of God even if he performs good deeds. It is after faith comes that good deeds are necessary.

> "And this is the condemnation, that light is come into the world, and men loved darkness rather than light, because their deeds were evil."
> John 3:19

When it says here that "men loved darkness rather than light," it means that they are more attached to the things of this world. They are more involved in the things of this world and are more interested in this sinful world. In the parable of the prodigal son, what did the younger son do? He had a complete change of heart as he realized that he would die of hunger if he carried on the way he was going. All that a person can do is turn around. That is repentance. It is all too easy to think, "All my life I've lived just as I pleased. Maybe it's time I started going to church," and to make this the first step to a reformed life. This is not, however, what is meant by repentance.

> I'm believing and receiving
> While I to the fountain go;
> And my heart the waves are cleansing
> Whiter than the driven snow.[15]

The faith that we come to know at that moment—the faith that enables us to entrust everything to God—is all-important. Entrusting everything to God is what is meant by receiving the light. In the world of nature there are bugs and winged insects that come thronging to the light. There appears to be a lesson for us to learn from this. Going to the kingdom of God is a matter of abiding in the light.

> Walking in sunlight all of my journey,
> Over the mountains, through the deep vale,
> Jesus has said, "I'll never forsake thee."
> Promise divine that never can fail.[16]

Jesus was "the true Light, which lighteth every man that cometh into the world" John 1:9. The moment we entrust ourselves to this true light, we are born anew as children of God.

He that Doeth Truth Cometh to the Light

> "For every one that doeth evil hateth the light, neither cometh to the light, lest his deeds should be reproved. But he that doeth truth cometh to the light, that his deeds may be made manifest, that they are wrought in God."
> John 3:20-21

Let's consider the relationship between parents and children. When a child does something wrong, if he admits to his parents what he has done and asks to be forgiven, in most cases the parents will forgive him. Even if the child has deceived his parents several times, if he is sorry and admits his fault, his parents cannot help but forgive him. In spite of their children's mistakes and wrongdoings, parents have a love for them that cannot be measured with money or other material goods. Doesn't everything else dissolve before this love?

There is a verse in the Bible that says:

> "For the law was given by Moses, but grace and truth came by Jesus Christ."
> John 1:17

In a way, this is similar to the love that parents have for their children. We were burdened every day by our sins. Our wrongdoings followed us everywhere, but then we were given a new strength. This strength is the light before which all sins dissolve. This happens in God, in the light. When the child of a household does something wrong the situation is different from when a servant does something wrong. Isn't it only natural for parents to forgive their child when he confesses his misdeeds? If there is still something in our hearts that constrains us, all we can do is confess it before God.

> "Blessed is he whose transgression is forgiven, whose sin is covered."
> Psalm 32:1

> "I acknowledged my sin unto thee, and mine iniquity have I not hid. I said, I will confess my transgressions unto the Lord; and thou forgavest the iniquity of my sin. Selah." Psalm 32:5

What words of blessing these are! I confessed all my sins before the Lord and He forgave me. He has pardoned me.

> "If we say that we have no sin, we deceive ourselves, and the truth is not in us. If we confess our sins, he is faithful and just to forgive us our sins, and to cleanse us from all unrighteousness. If we say that we have not sinned, we make him a liar, and his word is not in us." 1 John 1:8-10

These verses apply to those who have received eternal life. They have been given to us because they address a problem that arises in the lives of people who firmly believe that their sins have been forgiven. If we confess our wrongdoings and the sins that taint our daily lives, God forgives us.

> "My little children, these things write I unto you, that ye sin not. And if any man sin, we have an advocate with the Father, Jesus Christ the righteous: And he is the propitiation for our sins: and not for ours only, but also for the sins of the whole world." 1 John 2:1-2

He died not only for our sins, but for the sins of the whole world. "He that doeth truth cometh to the light, that his deeds may be made manifest, that they are wrought in God." John 3:21 Everything is forgiven that is wrought in God. Also, anyone who has not yet received forgiveness can be pardoned for all his sins when he comes to know the love of God. We believe that Jesus accomplished all things on the cross where He was sacrificed as the peace offering for our sins. The moment we come to this belief we receive peace in our hearts.

Herein Is Love

Not only has God given us rest, but His heart is also at rest and in peace in regard to us because we were lost, but now we have been found.

> "In this was manifested the love of God toward us, because that God sent his only begotten Son into the world, that we might live through him. Herein is love, not that we loved God, but that he loved us, and sent his Son to be the propitiation for our sins." 1 John 4:9-10

We often refer to the words that people say as "real gems," but are there any words more like a precious gemstone than these words of God? God sent His only begotten Son into the world so that we might live eternally. "Not that we loved God, but that he loved us." There is a hymn that says something similar to this:

> I've found a Friend, oh, such a Friend!
> He loved me 'ere I knew Him;
> He drew me with the cords of love,
> And thus He bound me to Him.[17]

This is the faith by which we live. There is also a hymn that includes the following lines:

> Let mock who may the way that you are taking,
> Be we but witnesses, confident and true.[18]

Wherein lies the confidence of a believer regarding his faith? If you ask someone who claims to believe, "How can you be so sure?" there will be some who will answer, "I have spoken in tongues," or "I have prophesied." But this is not the reason for our confidence. Neither is healing the sick evidence of faith. What is the evidence on which our faith is founded? First and foremost, it is the conviction that comes to the individual when he realizes that it was for his sins that Jesus, the Son of God, was crucified, died, was buried, and three days later rose from the dead.

> "If we receive the witness of men, the witness of God is greater: for this is the witness of God which he hath testified of his Son."
>
> 1 John 5:9

The witness of God is greater than any witness that man can give. Let's take a look at what this witness of God is.

> "He that believeth on the Son of God hath the witness in himself: he that believeth not God hath made him a liar." 1 John 5:10

Anyone who believes in God has the witness inside him. What is this witness? It is the belief that Jesus died for me, providing me with eternal redemption. Anyone who does not have this conviction, does not believe even though God has provided His witness. There is power at work within people who do not believe and this causes them to reject this witness, thinking, "God lied. His Son didn't die for me."

Those who believe, however, have the witness in themselves and so they do not make God out to be a liar. What is it that bears witness to the Son of God? It is faith in the fact that He died for my sins.

> "And this is the record, that God hath given to us eternal life, and this life is in his Son. He that hath the Son hath life; and he that hath not the Son of God hath not life." 1 John 5:11-12

> "He that hath the Son hath life; and he that hath not the Son of God hath not life."

Here we can see that there are those who have the Son and those who do not. Think about your own position. Which of these two groups do you belong to?

These Things I Have Written unto You

This faith gives us a certain comfort as we live our lives in this world. Even though we suffer, things do not seem so very bad. When we lose something, it does not seem such a great loss. Perhaps you have experienced this. Your heart is at peace, so you just take things as they come. Even though things may be difficult, it is better to live with faith than without. How could we live in the world, if we did not have this faith? If we did not have this conviction in our hearts, our lives would be empty and meaningless.

Why were we born? To breathe? To eat and drink? To wear nice clothes? To live somewhere a bit better than a hole in the wall? And after we die, is this all that will be written on our gravestones: "He ate, he lived, and he died"? Is this all we are living for?

Our lives on this earth may be short and humble, but we were born into this world in order to receive eternal life. We live with the hope that God's commandment will come upon us and when it does, we receive eternal life and go to stand before God.

> "These things have I written unto you that believe on the name of the Son of God; that ye may know that ye have eternal life, and that ye may believe on the name of the Son of God." 1 John 5:13

Even when things are explained clearly like this, there are still people who cannot believe. It is a really big problem when someone hears this message and still says that he has no idea what it all means.

Let's turn to John chapter 3 verse 21.

> "But he that doeth truth cometh to the light, that his deeds may be made manifest, that they are wrought in God."

This verse is talking about the actions that are carried out in the eternal God. Even people who have lived sinful lives know that they have been forgiven once they are in God. A person who has come to believe the truth knows that he has received eternal life.

> "He who believes in the Son has eternal life; but he who does not obey the Son shall not see life, but the wrath of God abides on him."
>
> John 3:36—NASV

"He who believes in the Son has eternal life; but he who does not obey the Son shall not see life." What does it mean to obey? Does obedience require the performing of good deeds? Or does it require faith? People standing under a roof do not get wet from the rain. A person who stands under a roof in the rain, but still puts up his umbrella just because it is new is a fool. As long as you are under the roof, you do not have to worry because the rain will fall on the roof and not on you. In much the same way, there is Someone who has taken our place and received the judgment that should have fallen on us. Jesus has taken our place and we are protected under Him.

> The trusting heart to Jesus clings,
> Nor any ill forebodes,
> But at the cross of Calvary sings,
> "Praise God for lifted loads!"
> Singing I go along life's road,
> Praising the Lord, praising the Lord;
> Singing I go along life's road,
> For Jesus has lifted my load.[19]

"But at the cross of Calvary sings, 'Praise God for lifted loads!'" This is quite amazing, isn't it? What would have become of us if it had not been for the cross of Jesus? If we had not been able to lay our burdens down at the foot of the cross and we were still carrying them around, how would we be able to live through all the troubles in our lives?

Fortunately, we have Someone who has lifted our loads and taken them upon Himself. Our burdens have been lifted before His cross. He has taken all our sins upon Himself and we simply need to be able to believe this in our hearts.

A Song that Looks to Eternity

Have you ever noticed a difference in the way you sing hymns now that you have come to believe in Jesus and the way you used to sing them?

> Savior, Savior, hear my humble cry;
> While on others Thou art calling,
> Do not pass me by.[20]

Perhaps you sang this hymn before you came to believe, and then there are the hymns we sing after we have come to believe.

> My Jesus, I love Thee, I know Thou art mine.
> For Thee all the follies of sin I resign.
> My gracious Redeemer, my Savior art Thou;
> If ever I loved Thee, my Jesus, 'tis now.
> ...
> And say when the death due lies cold on my brow;
> If ever I loved Thee, my Jesus, 'tis now.[21]

This is a hymn that looks to eternity. There is a clear distinction between hymns and other songs. In the past when I had no idea what the words of hymns were talking about, they did not seem to me to differ very much from any other songs, and they even seemed rather childish. My opinion changed, however, once I came to a definite realization of the love of God. There is a huge difference between hymns and the songs of this world.

> Once I was bound in the grip of all my sins.[22]

Originally there were very different words set to this music:

> Gone are the days when my heart was young and gay,
> Gone are my friends from the cotton fields away,
> Gone from the earth to a better land I know,
> I hear their gentle voices calling, "Old Black Joe."
> Why do I weep, when my heart should feel no pain,
> Why do I sigh that my friends come not again.[23]

Whenever I sang this song, my heart would be completely drawn into the nostalgia of it. The words would fill me with memories and longing for friends I had known in the past and lost. Such feelings used to preoccupy my heart, but now everything has changed.

> Once I was bound in the grip of all my sins,
> But then my Savior came and set me free.
> Although my sins were red as crimson bright,
> The blood of my dear Lord has washed them snowy white.
>
> I've cast aside all vain glory of the world
> And through God's grace many blessings now are mine,
> I give my heart and my body to the Lord,
> And serve Him in the glory of His heavenly home.
>
> Jesus Lord, Savior dear, for the sake of all my sins
> Was crucified and died upon the rugged cross.[24]

There's a world of difference between the two versions, isn't there? The original song expresses a longing for this world, a desire to see the people who are missed and far away. By contrast to this, the hymn talks of discarding vain glory. It tells how the fleeting things of this world will all disappear and how we have received many blessings through the grace of the Lord. The difference is that once we were in darkness but now we have come to see a brilliant light.

> "For God so loved the world, that he gave his only begotten Son, that whosoever believeth in him should not perish, but have everlasting life."
> John 3:16

This precious verse, John chapter 3 verse 16, can be seen as representative of the whole Bible. If it were not for the truth proclaimed in this verse, there would be no way for us to be saved. Jesus came to this world in order to offer His body as a sacrifice. God gave His only begotten Son for the sake of our sins. He prepared one eternal offering, Jesus, to keep us from being cast into hell. When He was nailed to the cross, He took upon Himself all of our sins. It was also in order that we might live eternally that Jesus rose from the dead. Some day our bodies will be changed to be like that of Jesus after His resurrection. He will return so that we can be clothed in such bodies of eternal life.

10

He Must Increase But I Must Decrease

John 3:22-4:2

The baptism given at the time of John the Baptist was
completely different from being baptized in the name of Jesus Christ.
John the Baptist administered the baptism of repentance,
but being baptized in the name of Jesus signifies
being buried with Jesus Christ
and being raised with Him from the dead.
This is the fundamental significance of baptism.

John 3:22-4:2

22After these things came Jesus and his disciples into the land of Judaea; and there he tarried with them, and baptized. 23And John also was baptizing in Aenon near to Salim, because there was much water there: and they came, and were baptized. 24For John was not yet cast into prison.

25Then there arose a question between some of John's disciples and the Jews about purifying. 26And they came unto John, and said unto him, Rabbi, he that was with thee beyond Jordan, to whom thou barest witness, behold, the same baptizeth, and all men come to him.

27John answered and said, A man can receive nothing, except it be given him from heaven. 28Ye yourselves bear me witness, that I said, I am not the Christ, but that I am sent before him. 29He that hath the bride is the bridegroom: but the friend of the bridegroom, which standeth and heareth him, rejoiceth greatly because of the bridegroom's voice: this my joy therefore is fulfilled. 30He must increase, but I must decrease. 31He that cometh from above is above all: he that is of the earth is earthly, and speaketh of the earth: he that cometh from heaven is above all. 32And what he hath seen and heard, that he testifieth; and no man receiveth his testimony. 33He that hath received his testimony hath set to his seal that God is true. 34For he whom God hath sent speaketh the words of God: for God giveth not the Spirit by measure unto him. 35The Father loveth the Son, and hath given all things into his hand. 36He that believeth on the Son hath everlasting life: and he that believeth not the Son shall not see life; but the wrath of God abideth on him.

4 1When therefore the Lord knew how the Pharisees had heard that Jesus made and baptized more disciples than John,

2(Though Jesus himself baptized not, but his disciples).

John the Baptist

This passage reveals very clearly what kind of a person John the Baptist was. It also expresses precisely the positions of these two persons—Jesus and John the Baptist.

John the Baptist was no ordinary person. I sometimes wonder what kind of person I would have been if I had been in his position. I could easily have become quite a contemptible person. What was John's position? He was born into this world in order to carry out one specific task: to bear witness to Jesus who would appear after him. In certain respects, it might seem as though Jesus usurped his position.

At such times, when one person becomes more popular than another, will the other person remain indifferent? In any country, even today, popularity is considered a matter of importance. When we were children, we, too, often wanted to stand out more than others. There are also times when we are jealous of others.

John the Baptist did not come in pursuit of power, wealth, or any other kind of personal gain. He did, however, have to face an important decision concerning his life. He chose to follow the course that had been set before him and not deviate from the path in the slightest. Let's take a look now at John's attitude.

In John chapter 3 verse 23 we read that when John was baptizing in Aenon near Salim, his disciples came to him and told him about what Jesus was doing.

"Teacher, that Man you were talking about is baptizing and many people are flocking to Him."

These words bring to mind the problems that have arisen between the various denominations ever since Christianity arose two thousand years ago, as each group has sought to win over more followers than the others. It has all been a question of whether one group has taken members from another group, or lost its members to another group. Ministers who have lost some of their members to another denomination have even been known to protest, "Why are you stealing my sheep?" Many denominations are concerned with such matters. It is a kind of war. In Europe, many people have died in wars that arose over matters of religion.

The attitude of John the Baptist, however, serves as a warning for the many religious leaders of this world, and it also provides a lesson for us individually. When competitiveness arises in our hearts, we need to consider whether it is well-intentioned, or whether it stems from a jealousy that will lead to hatred.

> "After these things came Jesus and his disciples into the land of Judaea; and there he tarried with them, and baptized. And John also was baptizing in Aenon near to Salim, because there was much water there: and they came, and were baptized." John 3:22-23

Here we can see that two great figures had come to the public eye: Jesus was baptizing and John the Baptist was also baptizing. In verse 22 it says, "After these things came Jesus and his disciples into the land of Judaea; and there he tarried with them, and baptized." Jesus Himself was not carrying out these baptisms. In John chapter 4 verse 2 it says, "Though Jesus himself baptized not, but his disciples." It was Jesus' disciples that were carrying out these baptisms. Since, at that time, the Holy Spirit had not yet come into the world, this baptism was different from the baptism we receive today in the name of the Father, the Son, and the Holy Spirit. The Holy Spirit came much later. Jesus was crucified and He died. He rose from the dead and revealed Himself to His disciples over a period of forty days before ascending into heaven. Then, ten days after that, on the day of Pentecost, the Holy Spirit came down to this earth.

So the baptism administered by Jesus' disciples at that time and the baptism given by John the Baptist were essentially the same. The work that John had been doing was passed over to Jesus' side. This was in accordance with an unspoken command of God. Even though Jesus' disciples were baptizing at that time, they did not really know who Jesus was. They did not know with any certainty that Jesus was the Son of God and the Christ.

The Last Prophet of Old Testament Times

> "For John was not yet cast into prison." John 3:24

Why does this verse say that John had not yet been thrown into prison? John was still carrying out his work, but before long, he would be locked up in prison and there he would die. John chapter 3 verse 25 tells us that a dispute arose between John's disciples and some of the Jews about the matter of purification.

> "Then there arose a question between some of John's disciples and the Jews about purifying." John 3:25

They were disputing over which baptism was of more value, that of John the Baptist or that of Jesus. They were arguing over which baptism was better. At that time, John's disciples came to him and told him that all the people were going to Jesus.

> "And they came unto John, and said unto him, Rabbi, he that was with thee beyond Jordan, to whom thou barest witness, behold, the same baptizeth, and all men come to him." John 3:26

People had come flocking to John the Baptist, but now they were all going to Jesus. Chapter 4 verses 1 and 2 tell us something similar.

> "When therefore the Lord knew how the Pharisees had heard that Jesus made and baptized more disciples than John, (Though Jesus himself baptized not, but his disciples)." John 4:1-2

More people were coming to Jesus' disciples to be baptized than to John the Baptist. If it had only been one person baptizing on each side, you might expect the numbers to be similar. While John was baptizing on his own, however, several of Jesus' disciples were all working together, and so it might have appeared that more people were being baptized by them. This work of God began shortly before John the Baptist had completed his course and was put to death. God knew all of this. Not too much later, John the Baptist would be beheaded.

John the Baptist's work was to bear witness to Jesus and to bring people to repentance. As the last prophet of Old Testament times, John the Baptist came to bear witness of Jesus. As the Old Testament prophets had written, he was sent ahead of Jesus and he came baptizing. This was the baptism of repentance. The preparations were being made for the work of God that would later be revealed through Jesus.

John the Baptist's disciples, however, became indignant. This man Jesus, who Himself had come to their teacher to be baptized, was now baptizing others and many people were going to Him! You can understand the exasperation of John's disciples, can't you? They thought that their teacher was the greatest, but now his popularity had declined. Let's take another look at the attitude of John's disciples here in verse 26.

> "And they came unto John, and said unto him, Rabbi, he that was with thee beyond Jordan, to whom thou barest witness, behold, the same baptizeth, and all men come to him."

Here John is addressed as "Rabbi," or teacher, while Jesus is simply referred to as "he" or "him." There is no sign of respect toward Jesus in these words; to them He was just a man. They saw John as their teacher and were upset that people were going to this other man to be baptized.

Except It be Given Him From Heaven

> "John answered and said, A man can receive nothing, except it be given him from heaven."
> John 3:27

Let's think about this. What have we come into this world to receive? What have we come to gain? In the book of Ecclesiastes it says:

> "The eye is not satisfied with seeing, nor the ear filled with hearing."
> Ecclesiastes 1:8

If you think about it, we eat and then we eat again; there is no end to our eating. It is the same when it comes to the clothes we wear. Perhaps clothes stay with us a little longer, since we even wear them when we are buried. Even so, once we die, our bodies rot and decompose. Death is the separation of the spirit and the body. In view of all this, can we claim to have gained anything in our lives?

From time to time, archeologists discover the tombs of ancient kings and in them they come across the hilts and sheaths of swords embellished with vast amounts of gold, but the blades have rusted so the swords can no longer be drawn from their sheaths. They also discover royal crowns in these tombs. These are all the kinds of items you might find on display in a museum. Even though the heads of these kings were adorned with many jewels as they were laid in their tombs, they did not take these treasures with them. Their bodies have decayed and are no more, and only their crowns remain above the place where their heads once laid.

Here in verse 27 it says, "John answered and said, A man can receive nothing, except it be given him from heaven." This verse tells us that, rather than material possessions, prestige, and the other things that the people of this world pursue, there is something eternal that we need to receive.

There is a preparation process through which a person must go before he dies in order to receive something that is given from heaven. In this respect, the baptism referred to here is extremely important.

As John the Baptist bore witness of Jesus, he left behind a tremendous lesson for his disciples. He taught them that his work in leading people to repentance was important, but that the work of Jesus was far greater. He taught them that Jesus' work would not be possible unless it had been given to Him from heaven.

He Who Was Sent Before Him

> "Ye yourselves bear me witness, that I said, I am not the Christ, but that I am sent before him." John 3:28

Let's take a careful look at this verse. Did John the Baptist say that he was the Christ, or that he was not the Christ? He said:

> "Ye yourselves bear me witness, that I said, I am not the Christ, but that I am sent before him."

John the Baptist was not concerned about the fact that he was being reduced to a subordinate position. In him we see the attitude of a man who had come to bear witness to the Christ. He taught his disciples that they were the ones who were to bear witness to his words.

"I am the one who has been sent before the Christ," he told them. "I am the one who has come to bear witness to the Christ before He appears. And you who have heard my sermons are the ones who are to bear witness to my words."

What was John's attitude? He put himself in a thoroughly humble position before Jesus. Why did John the Baptist come into the world? Let's take John chapter 1 verses 6 through 8 as one paragraph and see how the position of John the Baptist is completely disclosed here. Why did he come into this world?

> "There was a man sent from God, whose name was John. The same came for a witness, to bear witness of the Light, that all men through him might believe. He was not that Light, but was sent to bear witness of that Light."
> John 1:6-8

"There was a man sent from God." Who was this? It was John the Baptist, the man who came baptizing, wasn't it? "The same came for a witness." Of what did he come to bear witness? He bore witness of the Light. And who is this Light? It is Jesus. As we read through John's Gospel, we find Jesus Himself saying, "I am the light of the world" John 8:12. John the Baptist came with the aim of bearing witness of this Light so that all might come to believe in Jesus through him, that is, through John the Baptist. John the Baptist was the man who came to bear witness of Jesus.

Let's think of it this way. Suppose a little boy is planning to go on a school picnic. On the day of the picnic, he gets his lunch box ready and opens the door to go out only to find that it is raining outside. He remembers the words of his teacher the day before: "If it rains, we won't go."

In his frustration, he flings down his packed lunch and goes back into his room to sulk. He scribbles on the floor, stamps his feet, and throws things around. If it hadn't been for this rain he would have been at the picnic, having a good time with his friends. He is very disappointed. But then someone comes and taps the child on the shoulder and says, "Hey, it's stopped raining, and the sun has come out. Go and see."

If this person is someone who has always been honest with him, the child will say, "Okay," and run outside. If, on the other hand, this person has always been dishonest and mean to him, do you think the child will take any notice of him? He'll probably say something like, "Are you trying to trick me again?" The character of the person who delivers the message makes a great difference. If the child does not believe what this person says or does not respond to his words, will he look to see the light outside? He won't, will he? In a similar way, since John the Baptist had come to bear witness of the Light, his character was extremely important.

All of mankind was going along a certain path. Let me ask you something. What have we come into the world to do? Someone who loves eating may seem to have been born to eat; a person who dresses well may seem to have been born to wear nice clothes; and someone who loves movies may seem to have been born to watch movies. They all seem to have a purpose in life.

In reality, however, most people live in this world without knowing why they have been born, although they may find a purpose or create one for themselves later in life. But there was one man who was born with a purpose. That man was John the Baptist. He was born with a very clear purpose in life.

> "There was a man sent from God, whose name was John. The same came for a witness, to bear witness of the Light, that all men through him might believe."
> John 1:6-7

How many people have been born into this world with such a clear purpose?

After Me Cometh a Man

> "He that hath the bride is the bridegroom: but the friend of the bridegroom, which standeth and heareth him, rejoiceth greatly because of the bridegroom's voice: this my joy therefore is fulfilled. He must increase, but I must decrease."
> John 3:29-30

At a Jewish wedding, it was customary for the friends of the bridegroom to escort the bride to the groom. The friends of the groom rejoiced greatly as they brought the bride and handed her over to her husband. John the Baptist experienced that same joy felt by the friends of the groom. Is this a joy that just anyone can experience?

Suppose there are a group of young men, perhaps they all work in the same place or all go to the same synagogue. They are friends, but they all fall for the same beautiful young woman. In the end, the woman chooses one of them and the two marry. On the wedding day, how many of the other young men will truly be filled with joy as they honor the groom and deliver the bride to him?

But how did John the Baptist feel?

"He that hath the bride is the bridegroom." The one who has the bride will be extremely happy, but what about the others? "But the friend of the bridegroom, which standeth and heareth him, rejoiceth greatly because of the bridegroom's voice: this my joy therefore is fulfilled."

Perhaps this is rather difficult to understand. Why did John the Baptist compare Jesus to a bridegroom, and himself to the friends of the bridegroom who rejoice at the wedding? Why did he express it in this way?

"He must increase, but I must decrease."

He was saying, "Jesus must be glorified and exalted, but I must withdraw," in other words, "I must fade away." Could anyone adopt such an attitude through his own human strength?

It is possible that this feeling may arise within a person who, for example, hates someone, but then suddenly one day comes to know the gospel and believes that Jesus Christ is his Savior. A woman who cannot stand her mother-in-law may find that the moment she comes to know God's love, all these feelings of hatred disappear. Then when she hears the words, "Believe on the Lord Jesus Christ, and thou shalt be saved, and thy house" Acts 16:31, she feels excited as the desire arises within her to spread the gospel to her mother-in-law and the other members of her family. But after a while, the feelings of hatred return to her heart. Man's inner nature becomes exposed. We cannot help being the way we are, can we? The writer of the following hymn expressed this very well.

Helpless, guilty, hopeless, I lie.[1]

When John the Baptist said, "He that hath the bride is the bridegroom: but the friend of the bridegroom which standeth and heareth him, rejoiceth greatly," he was not referring to the feelings that arise between people in human society, feelings such as envy and jealousy. What was John the Baptist's purpose in coming into the world?

Let's turn to Mark chapter 1.

"The beginning of the gospel of Jesus Christ, the Son of God; As it is written in the prophets, Behold, I send my messenger before thy face, which shall prepare thy way before thee. The voice of one crying in the wilderness, Prepare ye the way of the Lord, make his paths straight. John did baptize in the wilderness, and preach the baptism of repentance for the remission of sins. And there went out unto him all the land of Judaea, and they of Jerusalem, and were all baptized of him in the river of Jordan, confessing their sins. And John was clothed with camel's hair, and with a girdle of a skin about his loins; and he did eat locusts and wild honey; And preached, saying, There cometh one mightier than I after me, the latchet of whose shoes I am not worthy to stoop down and unloose. I indeed have baptized you with water: but he shall baptize you with the Holy Ghost." Mark 1:1-8

The position of John the Baptist is clearly revealed in these verses. John quotes here from a verse in the book of Isaiah.

> "The voice of him that crieth in the wilderness, Prepare ye the way of the Lord, make straight in the desert a highway for our God."
>
> Isaiah 40:3

The words, "Behold, I send my messenger before thy face," come from Malachi chapter 3 verse 1.

> "Behold, I will send my messenger, and he shall prepare the way before me: and the Lord, whom ye seek, shall suddenly come to his temple, even the messenger of the covenant, whom ye delight in: behold, he shall come, saith the Lord of hosts."

The prophet Malachi had referred to "my messenger" many years earlier, and now John the Baptist was the one who came in that position. He was the one who came to prepare the way of the Lord. It was prophesied hundreds of years in advance that such a messenger would come, and that he would prepare the way of the Lord. He came to bear witness of the Christ.

The Friend of the Bridegroom Rejoiceth Greatly Because of the Bridegroom's Voice

There was a covenant that God had made with the Israelites over a long period of time. Among the Ten Commandments God gave to the Israelites, there was one that said, "Thou shalt have no other gods before me," and another that said, "Thou shalt not commit adultery." These commandments were not intended simply to teach them the moral standards by which they were to live.

If you look at the history of the Jews, you will find that there were many times when this nation turned away from God. They did not remain faithful to God, and therefore the Bible likens them to an adulteress. The Bible tells us again and again how the Jews were unfaithful to God when they should have considered Him their husband, and how they turned instead to worship gentile gods or allowed their hearts to be caught up in the ways of the Gentiles. It was the role of John the Baptist to bring to repentance the nation of Israel that had gone so far astray, and lead her back to her bridegroom. John the Baptist completed his mission. In Second Corinthians chapter 11 it says:

> "Would to God ye could bear with me a little in my folly: and indeed bear with me. For I am jealous over you with godly jealousy: for I have espoused you to one husband, that I may present you as a chaste virgin to Christ." 2 Corinthians 11:1-2

These words are addressed to the Church. When Paul wrote to the believers, "That I may present you as a chaste virgin to Christ," it means those who believe in Jesus Christ are to be presented before Him as His bride.

> "For thy Maker is thine husband; the Lord of hosts is his name; and thy Redeemer the Holy One of Israel; The God of the whole earth shall he be called. For the Lord hath called thee as a woman forsaken and grieved in spirit, and a wife of youth, when thou wast refused, saith thy God. For a small moment have I forsaken thee; but with great mercies will I gather thee. In a little wrath I hid my face from thee for a moment; but with everlasting kindness will I have mercy on thee, saith the Lord thy Redeemer." Isaiah 54:5-8

The "woman forsaken," the "wife of youth," is the nation of the Israelites. Passages that refer to the Israelites as a solitary woman or an unchaste woman appear throughout the Old Testament. Just as the prophets continually rebuked the Israelites for leaving the one and only God and living as they pleased, John the Baptist faithfully carried out the work of changing the hearts of the Israelites and presenting them to Christ. In Hosea chapter 2 it says:

"And I will betroth thee unto me for ever; yea, I will betroth thee unto me in righteousness, and in judgment, and in lovingkindness, and in mercies. I will even betroth thee unto me in faithfulness: and thou shalt know the Lord." Hosea 2:19-20

These words are addressed to the Israelites.

"'And it shall be, in that day,' Says the Lord, 'That you will call Me "My Husband."'" Hosea 2:16—NKJV

It says here that in that day the Israelites will call God their Husband. Also, in the verse we read from Second Corinthians chapter 11, the apostle Paul clearly says, "I have espoused you to one husband, that I may present you as a chaste virgin to Christ." So we can well understand the heart of John the Baptist who had finished his course and completed all the work that had been set before him.

"He that hath the bride is the bridegroom: but the friend of the bridegroom, which standeth and heareth him, rejoiceth greatly because of the bridegroom's voice: this my joy therefore is fulfilled. He must increase, but I must decrease." John 3:29-30

Here we have an expression of the heart of a man who is full of the joy of bearing witness to Christ. As you read these verses, perhaps you are reminded of one of the letters of the apostle Paul. He also wrote about having finished the course that he was to run.

"For we preach not ourselves, but Christ Jesus the Lord; and ourselves your servants for Jesus' sake. For God, who commanded the light to shine out of darkness, hath shined in our hearts, to give the light of the knowledge of the glory of God in the face of Jesus Christ." 2 Corinthians 4:5-6

Paul made his position very clear when he said, "We preach not ourselves." When Paul preached, he did not refer to his own authority or the greatness of his sermons; he simply explained about Christ. In his desire for the message he preached to be proclaimed in the correct manner, Paul assumed the attitude of a servant. He did not attempt to exalt himself over other people; he provided a model just as John the Baptist did.

One Great Among Them that Are Born of Women

When speaking of John the Baptist, Jesus said, "Among them that are born of women there hath not risen a greater than John the Baptist" Matthew 11:11. He was speaking of John's position and He said that he was a man greater than any other. We were all born of women, but there has never been anyone greater than John.

> "Verily I say unto you, Among them that are born of women there hath not risen a greater than John the Baptist: notwithstanding he that is least in the kingdom of heaven is greater than he. And from the days of John the Baptist until now the kingdom of heaven suffereth violence, and the violent take it by force. For all the prophets and the law prophesied until John. And if ye will receive it, this is Elias, which was for to come." Matthew 11:11-14

Here it says, "For all the prophets and the law prophesied until John." From this we can see that John the Baptist was a man of Old Testament times. Also, there has never been anyone born of woman that was greater than John the Baptist.

Everyone who has ever been born of a woman on this earth has been full of faults. If John the Baptist received a perfect score, what kind of score would we get? Our faults may not show on the outside, but when we delve deep inside ourselves, everything becomes exposed. We may greet someone with a smile, for example, even though we are cursing him inside. We have all kinds of evil inside us.

John the Baptist, on the other hand, was very pure. He did not need to fight with anyone to get food for himself; he lived on wild honey and locusts from the fields. It seems that there was an abundance of wild honey in those days. John was probably very healthy and had little need for money. Also, since he clothed himself in garments of camel's hair, he would have had no need to worry about what he was going to wear. Here was a man who lived with the sky as the roof over his head. He was a pure man, he kept every aspect of the law, and as a human being there was no one greater than he. This was no ordinary man. He also came from a very good family. His father was a priest who served God in the temple. His parents were such good people that Luke's Gospel describes them as being righteous before God.

> "There was in the days of Herod, the king of Judaea, a certain priest named Zacharias, of the course of Abia: and his wife was of the daughters of Aaron, and her name was Elisabeth. And they were both righteous before God, walking in all the commandments and ordinances of the Lord blameless. And they had no child, because that Elisabeth was barren, and they both were now well stricken in years."
> Luke 1:5-7

The child who was later born to this couple was John the Baptist. We have already discussed John's character and his activities, but the passage above describes the background of his birth. He was born into a truly great family. It even says that his parents were righteous before God. This is how pure his lineage was. His was a family of which to be proud.

I Must Decrease

Even though John the Baptist was such a great man, a person who is born of God is on a fundamentally different level.

"Which were born, not of blood, nor of the will of the flesh, nor of the will of man, but of God." John 1:13

It is useless to try to bring family lineage or breeding into this matter. Are we Jews? Are we descendants of Abraham? We aren't, are we? Some people pride themselves in the fact that their family has been Christian for many generations, or, for example, that their generation was the third in their family to receive infant baptism. "My grandfather is a pastor," they may boast. "And my father is a deacon." They are very proud of their family line. But those who are born of God are not born of blood, or of the will of the flesh, or of the will of man.

Jesus said, "Verily, verily, I say unto you, Except a corn of wheat fall into the ground and die, it abideth alone: but if it die, it bringeth forth much fruit" John 12:24. In a similar way, Jesus died on the cross and rose from the dead, and it is by faith in Jesus, the only begotten Son of God, that we become children of God. When we come to believe in Him we are changed. Isn't it better to be born of God than to be born of woman? Thus it is better to be in the position of a child of God than to be in the position of John the Baptist.

In John chapter 3 verse 30, John the Baptist made his position clear when he said, "He must increase, but I must decrease." This was in reply to his disciples' report that fewer people were coming to him and more were going to Jesus. As death lay right ahead of John the Baptist, he said, "He must increase, but I must decrease." .

The Baptism of John

Let's take a look at the approach taken by the Christians in the early church.

> "And a certain Jew named Apollos, born at Alexandria, an eloquent man, and mighty in the scriptures, came to Ephesus. This man was instructed in the way of the Lord; and being fervent in the spirit, he spake and taught diligently the things of the Lord, knowing only the baptism of John. And he began to speak boldly in the synagogue: whom when Aquila and Priscilla had heard, they took him unto them, and expounded unto him the way of God more perfectly."
>
> Acts 18:24-26

This is a really interesting story. This man by the name of Apollos was a learned person and was well-acquainted with the Old Testament scriptures. When it says, "This man was instructed in the way of the Lord," it means that he had made an extensive study of the Old Testament. "He spake and taught diligently the things of the Lord, knowing only the baptism of John." Even though Apollos used the Old Testament to explain to people who Jesus was, he was familiar only with the baptism of John. He did not know anything about being baptized "in the name of the Father, the Son, and the Holy Spirit." Neither did he know about the Holy Spirit entering a person's heart when that person comes to a firm belief in Jesus. He only knew the Old Testament as doctrinal teachings.

But then there was a faithful couple, Priscilla and Aquila. They were tentmakers and at one time they worked together with the apostle Paul.

> "And he began to speak boldly in the synagogue: whom when Aquila and Priscilla had heard, they took him unto them, and expounded unto him the way of God more perfectly."
>
> Acts 18:26

This couple, Priscilla and Aquila, heard Apollos preach and they must have spoken to each other about him. "Let's invite him to our house today and tell him more about Jesus." They took him into their house and began to talk to him. As they explained all about Jesus to him in detail, Apollos' eyes were opened.

> "And when he was disposed to pass into Achaia, the brethren wrote, exhorting the disciples to receive him: who, when he was come, helped them much which had believed through grace: For he mightily convinced the Jews, and that publickly, shewing by the scriptures that Jesus was Christ." Acts 18:27-28

Apollos bore witness of Jesus, explaining that He was the Christ who appeared in the Jewish scriptures—the Old Testament.

> "And it came to pass, that, while Apollos was at Corinth, Paul having passed through the upper coasts came to Ephesus: and finding certain disciples, He said unto them, Have ye received the Holy Ghost since ye believed? And they said unto him, We have not so much as heard whether there be any Holy Ghost. And he said unto them, Unto what then were ye baptized? And they said, Unto John's baptism. Then said Paul, John verily baptized with the baptism of repentance, saying unto the people, that they should believe on him which should come after him, that is, on Christ Jesus. When they heard this, they were baptized in the name of the Lord Jesus." Acts 19:1-5

In whose name did they now receive baptism? They were baptized in the name of Jesus. When people came to realize and believe firmly that Jesus was the Christ who appears in the Old Testament, the desire to be baptized before the Lord arose in their hearts.

Baptism in the Name of Jesus

The baptism received in the name of Jesus is not the same as the baptism that was given by John the Baptist. The baptism of John was the baptism for the repentance of sins, but the baptism received in the name of Jesus also signifies that we have died with Jesus.

> "Moreover, brethren, I would not that ye should be ignorant, how that all our fathers were under the cloud, and all passed through the

sea; And were all baptized unto Moses in the cloud and in the sea; And did all eat the same spiritual meat; And did all drink the same spiritual drink: for they drank of that spiritual Rock that followed them: and that Rock was Christ." 1 Corinthians 10:1-4

When the Israelites came out of Egypt, the pillar of cloud led them and the waters of the Red Sea parted before them. The Egyptians followed right behind them and drowned in the sea, but the Israelites passed through the waters and went up onto the land on the other side. This passage demonstrates how the former man, who belongs to Egypt, is buried under the water, and a new man comes to life. As the former man is submerged in the water and is then raised from the water in baptism, it represents death and resurrection. It signifies that he has died with Jesus and has been made alive again with Him. The same applies to us. The process by which we are saved is exactly the same.

> "The like figure whereunto even baptism doth also now save us (not the putting away of the filth of the flesh, but the answer of a good conscience toward God,) by the resurrection of Jesus Christ."
>
> 1 Peter 3:21

Baptism is "not the putting away of the filth of the flesh," but the first step of a good conscience toward God.

> "Know ye not, that so many of us as were baptized into Jesus Christ were baptized into his death? Therefore we are buried with him by baptism into death: that like as Christ was raised up from the dead by the glory of the Father, even so we also should walk in newness of life. For if we have been planted together in the likeness of his death, we shall be also in the likeness of his resurrection: Knowing this, that our old man is crucified with him, that the body of sin might be destroyed, that henceforth we should not serve sin. For he that is dead is freed from sin."
>
> Romans 6:3-7

Here again we can see that the baptism given at the time of John the Baptist was completely different from being baptized in the name of Jesus Christ. John the Baptist administered the baptism of repentance, but being baptized in the name of Jesus signifies being buried with Jesus Christ.

Colossians chapter 2 verse 12 expresses the fundamental meaning of baptism when it says, "[Ye are] buried with him in baptism, wherein also ye are risen with him." Also, in Acts chapter 2 we find the following passage:

> "Then Peter said unto them, Repent, and be baptized every one of you in the name of Jesus Christ for the remission of sins, and ye shall receive the gift of the Holy Ghost. For the promise is unto you, and to your children, and to all that are afar off, even as many as the Lord our God shall call."
> Acts 2:38-39

In whose name does it say that they were to be baptized?

"In the name of Jesus Christ."

None of the baptisms previously administered had been carried out in the name of Jesus.

Even today, the word "baptism" is often used. Baptism means to be immersed in water. In the history of the Church, there has long been a dispute over the matter of baptism.[2] People have argued over whether believers should be baptized by full immersion or simply christened with the sprinkling of a few drops of water. This argument has been going on for a long time although it rarely seems to come up these days.

Let's think about this matter a little more. Did the thief crucified next to Jesus have time to be baptized? Even though he was not baptized, he still went to paradise. So it seems that in cases where baptism is simply not possible, it is acceptable for a person to do without it.

Suppose a person meets a pastor on a plane. The pastor explains the gospel to him and he comes to believe in Jesus. If the plane then, for some reason, suddenly explodes in midair, would the new believer have time to be baptized?

If they were thrown from the plane as they flew over some water, perhaps the pastor could grab the man as they fell and say, "I baptize you in the name of the Father, the Son, and the Holy Spirit," but that is not very likely to happen, is it?

He That Cometh From Above

> "He that cometh from above is above all: he that is of the earth is earthly, and speaketh of the earth: he that cometh from heaven is above all." John 3:31

Here, when it says, "He that cometh from above," who is it talking about? The only person who has ever come from above is Jesus. Every member of the human race has been born of the earth, including John the Baptist. This verse bears witness of Jesus, the One who came from above.

> "Who is the image of the invisible God, the firstborn of every creature: For by him were all things created, that are in heaven, and that are in earth, visible and invisible, whether they be thrones, or dominions, or principalities, or powers: all things were created by him, and for him: And he is before all things, and by him all things consist." Colossians 1:15-17

He was the firstborn of every creature. He was before all things and He is above all things.

> "And what he hath seen and heard, that he testifieth; and no man receiveth his testimony." John 3:32

Jesus came from above and explained many things, but people did not yet know that they had to receive them. They did not even know how to receive them. For this reason, Jesus later said to Peter:

> "When thou art converted, strengthen thy brethren." Luke 22:32

He said, "When thou art converted." As Peter was following Jesus around, he made all kinds of vows, but Jesus did not believe Peter's words. He knew that it would not be long before Peter betrayed Him. First the Holy Spirit had to come. When the One who had come from heaven ascended there once more, the Holy Spirit would come down. Only then would people be able to receive the Holy Spirit, change their ways, and carry out the work that the Holy Spirit wanted them to do. Until that time, no one received His testimony because they did not understand it.

> "He that hath received his testimony hath set to his seal that God is true." John 3:33

There is a tendency for those who receive His testimony to react verbally with something like, "Oh, I see!" thus confirming what they have come to believe.

Sometimes when something is delivered to us, we have to sign a document to confirm that we have received it. Many years ago a personal seal would be used instead of a signature. The seal or the signature signifies a confirmation.

He That Believeth on the Son Hath Everlasting Life

> "For he whom God hath sent speaketh the words of God: for God giveth not the Spirit by measure unto him." John 3:34

All the Old Testament prophets continually wrote about God's salvation as they recorded the Scriptures, but the Holy Spirit that came upon them at that time was granted so that they could perform a specific task. In other words, the Holy Spirit appeared to them in order to use them for a specific task. Here in verse 34, however, it says, "God giveth not the Spirit by measure unto him." The Spirit itself is the life that God gives to us.

> "The Father loveth the Son, and hath given all things into his hand."
> John 3:35

The Father loves the Son and to whom has He given all things? Who has all authority? If you read through Psalm 2, you will find that everything falls into place. All the nations under heaven belong to Jesus Christ, the Son of God. Someday this will become a reality.

> "He that believeth on the Son hath everlasting life: and he that believeth not the Son shall not see life; but the wrath of God abideth on him."
> John 3:36

What does it say a person who believes on the Son has? He has "everlasting life." And what about the person who does not believe? He "shall not see life; but the wrath of God abideth on him."

This one verse divides the whole of mankind into two groups: those who will end up in hell and those who will end up in the kingdom of God. This is precisely the point. The whole of mankind, all the people who have ever been born in the history of the world, fall under one of these two categories: those who believe in the Son and those who do not. In other words, there are those who have eternal life, and those who do not. What becomes of those who do not believe, that is, those who do not obey? It says that the wrath of God abides on them, doesn't it? When I think about this it makes me shudder.

Let's think now about our children. In some way or other, parents may come to know and believe in the Bible but what will happen if they do not bring their children close to the Bible from an early age? What will abide on these children, if their parents do not lead them to faith in the Bible? The wrath of God will abide on them. This would be terrible! If a family member were to disappear one day, we would do all we could to find that person. What should we do then, if the spirits of those we love remain under the wrath of God? Can we live at peace with this? This is the responsibility of every believer.

God spoke in various ways to explain His method of redeeming the Israelites. The ways in which God reclaimed the Israelites, who were lost in their sin, explain the ways in which He saves man who is lost in sin. The Bible tells us, "For whatsoever things were written aforetime were written for our learning, that we through patience and comfort of the scriptures might have hope" Romans 15:4. It was written in order that we might follow in His footsteps.

> "For thus saith the Lord, Ye have sold yourselves for nought; and ye shall be redeemed without money."
> Isaiah 52:3

"Ye have sold yourselves for nought." How much did we pay in order to become sinners? It does not seem fair that we became sinners, after all it was Adam who sinned by eating the fruit of the tree of the knowledge of good and evil. This is why it says here, "Ye have sold yourselves for nought."

But it also says that we are redeemed without money. It is because Christ has paid the price for us with His blood that we have become children of God. We are able to go to the kingdom of God because Jesus has saved us. There are people who believe they will go to heaven because they have donated large sums of money to their church. Of course, making such donations is one way of expressing your gratitude to God.

> "He who believes in the Son has eternal life; but he who does not obey the Son shall not see life, but the wrath of God abides on him."
> John 3:36—NASV

When this verse says, "He who does not obey the Son," it does not refer to those people who disobey the various commandments given by the Son of God when He came to this earth. This does not mean disobedience in terms of actions; it means disobedience in terms of faith. It is a matter of not believing what you have been told to believe. It means that the wrath of God abides on him who does not believe the Son. Nothing else remains for such a person but to await God's judgment.

When we think about this, we ought to consider whether any members of our families or any of those around us do not yet believe in Jesus. We need to ask ourselves if the way we are living our daily lives or any of our faults is causing people around us to miss the opportunity to realize the truth of the gospel. It goes without saying that there is nothing in this world more precious than their spirits. If any member of our families does not find salvation because we have hurt them in some way or allowed ourselves to be upset by them, the responsibility falls upon us. This applies to every one of us. It is no use merely hoping for worldly success or gain for our families. Such things will not help them at all when it comes to receiving eternal life, since they cannot take any of those things with them when they die. For those who have received God's gift of eternal life, there will be no greater prize than to meet one another as they go through the doors to heaven and stand before God.

11

Living Water that Quenches Spiritual Thirst

John 4:3-19

Six husbands had not been able to quench the woman's thirst.
"Thirst" seems to be the best expression to use
in describing the deep distress inside of man.
The Samaritan woman was seeking a conclusive answer to life.
People are so busy with all their various activities and interests that they
are unaware of the thirst in their spirits; they have become numb to it.
It is a problem if a person has never had the thirst
that this woman was experiencing.

John 4:3-19

³He left Judaea, and departed again into Galilee. ⁴And he must needs go through Samaria. ⁵Then cometh he to a city of Samaria, which is called Sychar, near to the parcel of ground that Jacob gave to his son Joseph. ⁶Now Jacob's well was there. Jesus therefore, being wearied with his journey, sat thus on the well: and it was about the sixth hour. ⁷There cometh a woman of Samaria to draw water: Jesus saith unto her, Give me to drink. ⁸(For his disciples were gone away unto the city to buy meat.)

⁹Then saith the woman of Samaria unto him, How is it that thou, being a Jew, askest drink of me, which am a woman of Samaria? for the Jews have no dealings with the Samaritans.

¹⁰Jesus answered and said unto her, If thou knewest the gift of God, and who it is that saith to thee, Give me to drink; thou wouldest have asked of him, and he would have given thee living water.

¹¹The woman saith unto him, Sir, thou hast nothing to draw with, and the well is deep: from whence then hast thou that living water? ¹²Art thou greater than our father Jacob, which gave us the well, and drank thereof himself, and his children, and his cattle?

¹³Jesus answered and said unto her, Whosoever drinketh of this water shall thirst again: ¹⁴But whosoever drinketh of the water that I shall give him shall never thirst; but the water that I shall give him shall be in him a well of water springing up into everlasting life.

¹⁵The woman saith unto him, Sir, give me this water, that I thirst not, neither come hither to draw. ¹⁶Jesus saith unto her, Go, call thy husband, and come hither.

¹⁷The woman answered and said, I have no husband. Jesus said unto her, Thou hast well said, I have no husband: ¹⁸For thou hast had five husbands; and he whom thou now hast is not thy husband: in that saidst thou truly.

¹⁹The woman saith unto him, Sir, I perceive that thou art a prophet.

The Region of Samaria

The above passage is a record of a conversation that took place between Jesus and a woman of loose moral standards. At that time in Israel the people who lived in the region in which this incident took place were treated with the greatest of contempt. Jesus had to pass through this region. He was not there as a person who was treated with contempt by the local inhabitants; He was approaching a village in that area as one of those who scorned its people. This region was called Samaria.

Perhaps you have had this kind of experience. You are on your way somewhere and you come to a side street that you do not feel inclined to enter. It may be quicker to go that way, but you would rather not, so you choose to take a longer route. There will probably also be people who do not like to walk down a street that is lined with bars. When I was a child, there was a certain neighborhood that I never went anywhere near because the adults who frequented that street would rail any child that went there. I had no idea what actually went on there, but I always made a detour to avoid the area. This was probably because people said that neighborhood was full of people of socially undesirable character.

At the time of Jesus, the Jews, who prided themselves on being the descendants of Abraham, Isaac, and Jacob, did not even treat the Samaritans as human beings. In 722 B.C., the Northern Kingdom of Israel was destroyed and many people were taken as captives to Assyria.

Later, Samaria became full of people the Assyrians had driven out of other regions, and the Jews who had remained behind there intermarried with these Gentiles, leaving behind descendants of mixed blood.[1]

When the Israelites who had been in bondage in Egypt crossed the Red Sea and set out on their journey through the wilderness,

119

God commanded them not to enter into marriage with Gentiles. This was an ironclad law.

> "Neither shalt thou make marriages with them; thy daughter thou shalt not give unto his son, nor his daughter shalt thou take unto thy son. For they will turn away thy son from following me, that they may serve other gods: so will the anger of the Lord be kindled against you, and destroy thee suddenly." Deuteronomy 7:3-4

The Jews in the south adhered strictly to this law, but the Samaritans disobeyed and mixed with the Gentiles. As a result, the Jews came to treat the Samaritans as being less than human. They despised the Samaritans for many long years after this. Later, when the Jews returned to their homeland following their time of captivity in Babylon and were rebuilding the temple, the Samaritans offered their help, but the Jews refused them.[2]

Later, the Samaritans built a temple of their own, but the Jews destroyed that as well.[3] The two groups thus became sworn enemies who would have nothing to do with each other. Even to this day, there are Samaritans living in Israel as a minority race but their numbers are very small.

Jesus Saith unto Her, Give Me to Drink

Jesus, who was a Jew, came to be passing through Samaria, this land so despised by Jews. He could have proceeded directly from Judea to Galilee, but it seems that He probably traveled through Samaria in order to avoid running into any of the Jews or their religious leaders. Chapter 4 verses 3 and 4 describe His route:

> "He left Judaea, and departed again into Galilee. And he must needs go through Samaria." John 4:3-4

As Jesus was passing through this area, He sat down by a well. It would have been about noon in today's time and since it was the hottest time of the day, most people would have been indoors, so there was hardly anyone to be seen outside. Jesus' disciples had gone to buy some food, and Jesus was sitting alone by the well when a woman happened to appear, carrying her waterpot.

Nowadays, we only need to turn on the faucet in the kitchen to get some water. The source of the water may be miles away, but it will flow easily from the faucet even in an apartment at the top of a high-rise building. In biblical times, however, people had to walk to a well that was usually located outside the town.

This woman probably went to the well in the middle of the day like this in order to avoid the gaze of other people. No one else would have come to draw water at midday. Most people would have gone to the well in the cool of the morning or the evening. In any case, it seems that this was not a woman who felt she could hold her head up in the presence of other people. Since she tried to avoid meeting anyone when she came to the well, we can see that she was wary of the opinions of others. This woman came alone to draw water, but she happened to meet Jesus, and the two began to talk. Let's read on and see how the conversation between Jesus and this woman unfolded.

> "Then cometh he to a city of Samaria, which is called Sychar, near to the parcel of ground that Jacob gave to his son Joseph. Now Jacob's well was there. Jesus therefore, being wearied with his journey, sat thus on the well: and it was about the sixth hour. There cometh a woman of Samaria to draw water: Jesus saith unto her, Give me to drink. (For his disciples were gone away unto the city to buy meat.)"
> John 4:5-8

The woman was probably surprised to see Jesus sitting there. She had thought she would be alone at the well, but came upon this Jew, a man from a nation that scorned her people and treated them as less than human. She must have looked at Him in amazement. In any case, Jesus asked this woman He had never met before to give Him some water.

> "Then saith the woman of Samaria unto him, How is it that thou, being a Jew, askest drink of me, which am a woman of Samaria? for the Jews have no dealings with the Samaritans." John 4:9

The woman was startled that Jesus asked her for a drink. It completely perplexed her that a Jew had addressed her, a Samaritan, and asked for a drink of water. The Jews had nothing to do with Samaritans, so she said, "You're a Jew. Are You asking me, a Samaritan woman, for a drink?"

Shall Never Thirst Again

> "Jesus answered and said unto her, If thou knewest the gift of God, and who it is that saith to thee, Give me to drink; thou wouldest have asked of him, and he would have given thee living water." John 4:10

He had asked for some water, but now He started talking about something completely different. He said something the likes of which this woman had never heard in her life from anyone. In the conversation between these two people, an issue arose that no one had ever broached before. To put it simply, Jesus was saying, "If you knew who I was, you would ask Me for water." This woman's thoughts were far from what was in Jesus' heart. The difference between this woman's thoughts and those of Jesus was like the difference between heaven and earth. When Jesus said, "Thou wouldest have asked of him," it sounds as though He was talking about a third person, but He was actually referring to Himself. It was not as an ordinary man that He stood there before this woman.

> "If thou knewest the gift of God, and who it is that saith to thee, Give me to drink; thou wouldest have asked of him, and he would have given thee living water."
>
> John 4:10

Perhaps in the eyes of this Samaritan woman Jesus appeared as an ordinary Jew asking her for some water, but this was not the way it actually was. Jesus was a completely different being. He was speaking on a very different level from anything that this woman had in mind. Jesus began by saying, "If thou knewest the gift of God."

Who is this "gift of God"? At this time, Jesus was speaking from the point of view of God who is Father, Son, and Holy Spirit. He was speaking as the Son of God.

> "The woman saith unto him, Sir, thou hast nothing to draw with, and the well is deep: from whence then hast thou that living water?"
>
> John 4:11

Here when the woman addressed Jesus as, "Sir," it signifies that she was showing a little more respect for this Man who stood before her.

This woman had a waterpot and she probably had a well bucket as well. Jesus, on the other hand, had nothing at all. To the woman, He must have seemed pathetic. Quite out of the blue, He began to speak about "the gift of God," and said, "If thou knewest … who it is that saith to thee, Give me to drink; thou wouldest have asked of him, and he would have given thee living water." The woman thought of this living water as water drawn from the well with a bucket, so she asked:

> "Sir, thou hast nothing to draw with, and the well is deep: from whence then hast thou that living water? Art thou greater than our father Jacob, which gave us the well, and drank thereof himself, and his children, and his cattle?"
>
> John 4:11-12

"Our father Jacob gave this well to his children and we too have drunk from it." The sons of Jacob raised sheep and cattle, so they would have watered their animals at the well, wouldn't they? "Art thou greater than our father Jacob?"

> "Jesus answered and said unto her, Whosoever drinketh of this water shall thirst again. But whosoever drinketh of the water that I shall give him shall never thirst; but the water that I shall give him shall be in him a well of water springing up into everlasting life." John 4:13-14

Even though they drank the water from this well again and again, they still became thirsty. "But whosoever drinketh of the water that I shall give him shall never thirst."

The woman was astonished; she had met a very great Man. Every time she was thirsty she had to bring her waterpot and come to draw water, but this Man said that the water He gave would quench her thirst forever. He also said that it would become a well of the water within her springing up to eternal life.

> "The woman saith unto him, Sir, give me this water, that I thirst not, neither come hither to draw." John 4:15

"I won't have to come here ever again! I'll never be thirsty again! I won't need to come to draw water!" When the woman heard these amazing words from Jesus, she asked if she might also have some of this water. Now they had completely changed places. Who first asked for some water? It was Jesus, wasn't it? But now it was the other way around and the woman was asking for some water.

Go, Call Thy Husband, and Come Hither

> "Jesus saith unto her, Go, call thy husband, and come hither." John 4:16

Living Water that Quenches Spiritual Thirst

The woman had asked Jesus for water, but His reply was completely unexpected. He might have told her to fetch a container for the water, or to get a bigger waterpot, but all of a sudden He told her to go and get her husband. It might seem that Jesus was intending to give her this water in the presence of her husband because the woman might feel awkward in the company of a man she did not know, but this was not the case.

"The woman answered and said, I have no husband."   John 4:17

Jesus saw all that lay in the woman's heart as He told her to go and bring her husband. She was completely frank in her answer: "I have no husband."

"Jesus said unto her, Thou hast well said, I have no husband."
John 4:17

"It is really true that you have no husband. You are being honest." This is what He was saying.

"For thou hast had five husbands; and he whom thou now hast is not thy husband: in that saidst thou truly."   John 4:18

The apostle John wrote this account in a reserved style, but how would it be if we consider this story in a more emotional light?

This woman had crept along to the well at a time when no one was about, looking around to make sure she was not seen, only to find, when she got there, that a Jewish man was sitting by the well. This woman was scorned enough by her own neighbors, but now along came this Jew, a member of a nation that despises her whole nation. That alone had startled her enough, but this Man went on to ask for some water and then He promised to give her some water that would quench her thirst forever. When the woman asked for some of this water, Jesus told her to go and bring her husband. The woman said that she had no husband, and then what did Jesus say?

125

"You are absolutely right to say that you have no husband. You're being honest."

Why was this? Jesus explained:

"For thou hast had five husbands; and he whom thou now hast is not thy husband." John 4:18

What would have been the expression on this woman's face as these words of Jesus penetrated deep into her heart? No matter how great a mess she may have made of her life, she still had the vulnerable heart of a woman and Jesus had hit her most sensitive spot. Would she have remained unperturbed? If she had been a woman of our times, she might have sprung at Him, cursing Him for hurting her pride. Let's read this conversation once more.

"Jesus saith unto her, Go, call thy husband, and come hither. The woman answered and said, I have no husband. Jesus said unto her, Thou hast well said, I have no husband: For thou hast had five husbands; and he whom thou now hast is not thy husband: in that saidst thou truly." John 4:16-18

By this time, this woman would have been sweating from head to toe. The weather was hot enough if nothing else, so at that time of day she would have been sweating profusely. In addition to this, however, Jesus had laid bare all the secrets contained in this woman's heart. Let's take a look at how she reacted to this.

Thou Art a Prophet

"The woman saith unto him, Sir, I perceive that thou art a prophet." John 4:19

"Sir, I can see that You are a prophet. You are one of the prophets such as came to our ancestors long ago in the history of Israel."

In the next verse the woman went on to speak about the proper place to worship God. At this moment, there was a change of scene. Jesus' words had pierced this woman's conscience. In her desire to ease her troubled conscience, she brought up the matter of worshiping God. Jesus knew all her thoughts and what was in her heart. He knew why she suddenly began to speak of worship as she found herself having reached a dead end with no way of escape. Knowing what was in this woman's heart, Jesus led the conversation along.

Let's think about this woman. What kind of a woman was she? Some people may dismiss this loose woman as a flirt who had been through five husbands and make the big mistake of thinking that her story has nothing to do with their own situation. The distinction between men and women only applies in terms of outward appearance; we all experience the same internal struggles. We all become upset when people treat us with contempt and we all feel sorry for ourselves when people slight us.

Jesus said, "Thou hast had five husbands; and he whom thou now hast is not thy husband." These six husbands had not been able to quench the woman's thirst. "Thirst" seems to be the best expression to use in describing the deep distress inside of man. This was what the Samaritan woman was experiencing as she sought a conclusive answer to life.

> Fly as a bird to your mountain
> Thou who art weary of sin;
> Go to the clear flowing fountain
> Where you may wash and be clean.
>
> Fly forth, Avenger is near thee,
> Call, and the Saviour will hear thee,
> He on His bosom will bear thee
> Oh, thou who art weary of sin.[4]

Even if we have just been drinking some water, if someone makes a hurtful comment or insults us, it can be enough to make our throats grow parched. Our mouths become completely dry. Why is this? "Thirst" seems to be the word that best expresses the frustrations we experience in our spirits.

As is revealed in the fact that the Samaritan woman had had five husbands and the one she now had was not her own, this woman was experiencing spiritual thirst. Also, this thirst had extended into a physical thirst. She had gone to draw water to quench this thirst, when suddenly a Man appeared and said, "Give me to drink." These words indicate that Jesus was also thirsty. It was not only a physical thirst, however, that led Jesus to say these words. He began the conversation in this way with the aim of quenching the agony of the thirst deep in the woman's heart, using water from a new spring.

Give Me to Drink

Is there anything in this world that can quench the spiritual thirst from which we suffer? Haven't you already tried very hard in your life to fill the emptiness in your heart? Perhaps you have read many books, or watched many movies. You probably remember times when you have searched hard for something, without really knowing what it was. If you think back over your life from the time you were a child, you will probably be aware that you have always been searching for something in your heart, something beyond food to satisfy your hunger and drink to quench your thirst. We all experience this spiritual thirst because we are all thirsty.

This woman had had six husbands, but none of them had been able to bring her contentment. Similarly, there were six empty waterpots at the wedding feast that Jesus had attended in Cana of Galilee not long before this. It was only after Jesus had ordered the servants to fill the waterpots with water and changed the water into wine that a feeling of contentment flowed through the wedding feast. The number six signifies man, and the six empty waterpots indicates that the flesh can never be satisfied without the presence of God.

As Jesus spoke with this woman beside the well, He promised that He would give her eternal living water. This was a promise that would live on eternally within mankind, remaining valid even after this woman died. We cannot help but be reminded here of the scene after man was lost to sin. Man was driven out of the Garden of Eden and came to dwell in a desolate and parched land where he suffered endless thirst.

> "Thorns also and thistles shall it bring forth to thee; and thou shalt eat the herb of the field." Genesis 3:18

Mankind was thus driven out and scattered across the face of the earth on account of sin. It was in order to guide all of mankind back to Him, that Jesus was crucified on the hill called Golgotha. The hours of Jesus' suffering centered around twelve noon: He hung on the cross from 9 o'clock in the morning until 3 o'clock in the afternoon. For all those long hours He hung and suffered there.

Just before Jesus died, He said, "I thirst" John 19:28. At that time, some people soaked a sponge in vinegar, tied it to a branch of hyssop, and put it to His mouth. It was then that the words King David had written one thousand years earlier were fulfilled: "They gave me also gall for my meat; and in my thirst they gave me vinegar to drink" Psalm 69:21.

> "God, who at sundry times and in divers manners spake in time past unto the fathers by the prophets, hath in these last days spoken unto us by his Son." Hebrews 1:1-2

"His Son" had never received anything from anyone on this earth to quench His thirst until His final moments on the cross when He said, "It is finished" John 19:30. At the very end, when Jesus said He was thirsty, they brought some vinegar and put it to His lips. Even then He only accepted this to fulfill the prophecy recorded in the Scriptures.

Even as Jesus stood beside this well in Samaria, He was well aware of the crucifixion that lay ahead of Him. He knew what He would have to go through. He could even feel it and He thought ahead to it as He spoke with this woman. It was only after Jesus had died in this way that the eternal living water would flow from Him. Let's turn now to Matthew chapter 27 and read from verse 45.

> "Now from the sixth hour there was darkness over all the land unto the ninth hour. And about the ninth hour Jesus cried with a loud voice, saying, Eli, Eli, lama sabachthani? that is to say, My God, my God, why hast thou forsaken me? Some of them that stood there, when they heard that, said, This man calleth for Elias. And straightway one of them ran, and took a spunge, and filled it with vinegar, and put it on a reed, and gave him to drink."
> Matthew 27:45-48

Let's turn also to John's Gospel chapter 19 and read from verse 28.

> "After this, Jesus knowing that all things were now accomplished, that the scripture might be fulfilled, saith, I thirst. Now there was set a vessel full of vinegar: and they filled a spunge with vinegar, and put it upon hyssop, and put it to his mouth. When Jesus therefore had received the vinegar, he said, It is finished: and he bowed his head, and gave up the ghost."
> John 19:28-30

This was the scene that Jesus knew was coming, the final scene in which He would die not just for this Samaritan woman but also for all of mankind. He also knew that at that time He would say, "I thirst." This was why, when He spoke to the woman who had come to draw water from the well, He said, "Give me to drink." This is what He asks of the whole of mankind. There is nothing, however, that man can offer to Jesus. Man can do nothing for Him.

Was this just a chance meeting between Jesus and the woman? When Jesus was on His way to Galilee, why did He happen to go through this region that was despised by the Jews?

A Thirst for Hearing the Words of the Lord

We can think of it in this way. Jesus knew all about the path this woman was taking. She was walking through her own life—walking her own path—but at this moment in time, Jesus was matching His own eternal steps with the steps of this woman. Why did He do this? He did it for all those people who would later be born, live their fleeting lives in this world, and die thirsty. He left behind this lesson in order that He might give eternal life to all of mankind. Jesus came to find mankind. He, personally, had come in search of this woman. He had already known that she would come to the well at that hour and so He met her there. Let's think about this.

> "Behold, the days come, saith the Lord God, that I will send a famine in the land, not a famine of bread, nor a thirst for water, but of hearing the words of the Lord: And they shall wander from sea to sea, and from the north even to the east, they shall run to and fro to seek the word of the Lord, and shall not find it. In that day shall the fair virgins and young men faint for thirst." Amos 8:11-13

This passage speaks of a thirst that only the word of God can quench. There are people who are not aware of their own thirst or fatigue. There are also people who will wear thick winter clothes, with a warm hat pulled firmly down over their ears, and walk around the streets laughing even on a scorching hot day. People like this are out of their minds. Either they are suffering from malarial fever, or they must have no sense of feeling. There are also people who will walk around the streets on a freezing cold winter's day, laughing to themselves without a stitch of clothing on them. These people must also have no sense of feeling.

This is precisely the state of mankind, living as though unaware of God's word. Many people are caught up in the joys of the world. They are so busy with all their various activities and interests that they are unaware of the thirst in their spirits; they have become numb to it. This Samaritan woman had been treated very badly, but if she had not had the thirst she was experiencing, she would have had an even greater problem. This thirst comes to those who are searching for truth. Just as the Jews had fallen into this problem, everyone suffers from this spiritual thirst today since they have become separated from God and lost in sin. Everyone who is apart from God will inevitably feel this thirst.

> "They have dealt treacherously against the Lord: for they have begotten strange children: now shall a month devour them with their portions."
> Hosea 5:7

It says here, "They have dealt treacherously against the Lord." This is pointing out that man has departed from God and continually wanders lost, looking for something else, and trying to quench the thirst in his spirit with something else.

> "Ye adulterers and adulteresses, know ye not that the friendship of the world is enmity with God? whosoever therefore will be a friend of the world is the enemy of God."
> James 4:4

Here it says, "Ye adulterers and adulteresses." If we try to substitute the things of this world for the things of God, we will be reproached in this way when we stand before God.

This was precisely the position of this Samaritan woman. She had tried to quench her thirst with all sorts of things that had nothing to do with God, but in the end she had met a certain Person. First He asked her for something, didn't He? In the end, however, it was the woman who asked Him for something. None of man's religions, man's faith, or man's righteousness can be offered to God. He has already done everything for us.

In our main text we read that Jesus asked for a drink, but it does not say anywhere that He was given one and drank it, does it? Let's take another look at John chapter 4 verse 7.

> "There cometh a woman of Samaria to draw water: Jesus saith unto her, Give me to drink."

Jesus asked the Samaritan woman for a drink. This event took place long ago, but it provides exactly the same lesson for us today. Did God save us because He saw some special quality in us before we were saved? No, we had no such special quality at all. It was simply that He shone the light into darkness. We were the darkness, and He was the bright light. It was simply that the darkness was changed to light. Our darkness could not block this light. This woman could not give Jesus anything at all; she had nothing she could offer to Him. We are just the same as this woman when we stand before Jesus.

The Gift of God

Let's take a look at something Jesus said much later. It was forty days after He rose from the dead. When His disciples were gathered together, He said to them:

> "But ye shall receive power, after that the Holy Ghost is come upon you: and ye shall be witnesses unto me both in Jerusalem, and in all Judaea, and in Samaria, and unto the uttermost part of the earth."
>
> Acts 1:8

Then Jesus ascended into heaven. The Samaritans had an understanding of worship that seems to have enabled them to be a little closer to God than the Gentiles who knew nothing at all of God and therefore were unable to approach Him. Thus the Samaritans acted as a door for the Gentiles. They were a gateway through which the gospel would pass from the Jews to the Gentiles. Jesus explained to the Jews that the gospel would be spread in this way when He said, "Ye shall be witnesses unto me both in Jerusalem, and in all Judaea, and in Samaria, and unto the uttermost part of the earth."

Jesus said, "Whosoever drinketh of the water that I shall give him shall never thirst." We are born into this world as sinners, not knowing how to quench the thirst we feel inside, how we will spend our lives, when or how we will die, or where we will go after we die, but God has opened the door to us. Jesus came in advance to give us this gift in order to guide and receive us into His eternal kingdom.

Let's take another look now at this important point in verse 10.

"Jesus answered and said unto her, If thou knewest the gift of God."
John 4:10

"If thou knewest the gift of God." What is the greatest of all God's gifts? It is Jesus Himself.

"For God so loved the world, that he gave his only begotten Son."
John 3:16

If it were not for this gift, mankind would perish. Birth itself would be a curse. No matter how wealthy a household you were born into—even if you were born in a royal palace—it would be a curse to be brought into existence. But the gift of God has been given to us; God has given us the gift of His only begotten Son.

"That was the true Light, which lighteth every man that cometh into the world. He was in the world, and the world was made by him, and the world knew him not. He came unto his own, and his own received him not. But as many as received him, to them gave he power to become the sons of God, even to them that believe on his name." John 1:9-12

The children of God are those people who believe on His name and believe that He has given us this gift.

"Jesus answered and said unto her, If thou knewest the gift of God, and who it is that saith to thee, Give me to drink; thou wouldest have asked of him, and he would have given thee living water." John 4:10

Who was it that said, "Give me to drink"? It was Jesus, the Son of God. Jesus told the woman that if she had known who He was, she would have asked Him, and the Son of God would have given her living water. Jesus is the greatest gift in the world and He has been given to all of mankind, to each one of us individually.

There are very many people who think it is enough just to exchange cards and gifts at Christmas in memory of Jesus' birth, but that is not enough. The true gift is Jesus Himself, who came to this earth in order to save sinners. He came in order to pour out eternal living water upon the thirsty spirits of men. The important point is how we believe in Him.

The Samaritan woman said, "Sir, I perceive that thou art a prophet." This was because she had discovered the thirst in her spirit and was coming to know Jesus. The moment had come for her to seek the place where she could worship and there open her heart before God.

It is the same for us. We, too, need to cling to Jesus in our hearts as we think about Him. We need to find a place to sit down quietly and calmly to pray, "Lord, You must have had a purpose in saving me." As we pray in this way, the faith we received when we came to believe in Jesus may well up inside us once more as living water.

Since He is the well of living water, He has promised that a new change can arise in our hearts just as we experienced when we first came to know God's love.

12

The Essential Nature of Worship and the Eternal Harvest

John 4:20-42

Why have religions arisen within the human race?
When people's consciences are troubling them or they are suffering,
the first thing they turn to is religion.
The woman asked where she should worship.
This woman was searching for an object of worship.
Jesus answered her on an entirely different level.
"The hour cometh ... when the true worshippers
shall worship the Father in spirit and in truth."
Jesus was announcing here that through the guidance of the Holy Spirit,
people would begin to worship God in spirit.
There is no need here for any of man's efforts or strength.

John 4:20-42

[20] Our fathers worshipped in this mountain; and ye say, that in Jerusalem is the place where men ought to worship.

[21] Jesus saith unto her, Woman, believe me, the hour cometh, when ye shall neither in this mountain, nor yet at Jerusalem, worship the Father. [22] Ye worship ye know not what: we know what we worship: for salvation is of the Jews. [23] But the hour cometh, and now is, when the true worshippers shall worship the Father in spirit and in truth: for the Father seeketh such to worship him. [24] God is a Spirit: and they that worship him must worship him in spirit and in truth.

[25] The woman saith unto him, I know that Messias cometh, which is called Christ: when he is come, he will tell us all things.

[26] Jesus saith unto her, I that speak unto thee am he.

[27] And upon this came his disciples, and marvelled that he talked with the woman: yet no man said, What seekest thou? or, Why talkest thou with her?

[28] The woman then left her waterpot, and went her way into the city, and saith to the men,

[29] Come, see a man, which told me all things that ever I did: is not this the Christ? [30] Then they went out of the city, and came unto him.

[31] In the mean while his disciples prayed him, saying, Master, eat.

[32] But he said unto them, I have meat to eat that ye know not of.

[33] Therefore said the disciples one to another, Hath any man brought him ought to eat?

[34] Jesus saith unto them, My meat is to do the will of him that sent me, and to finish his work. [35] Say not ye, There are yet four months, and then cometh harvest? behold, I say unto you, Lift up your eyes, and look on the fields; for they are white already to harvest. [36] And he that reapeth receiveth wages, and gathereth fruit unto life eternal: that both he that soweth and he that reapeth may rejoice together. [37] And herein is that saying true, One soweth, and another reapeth. [38] I sent you to reap that whereon ye bestowed no labour: other men laboured, and ye are entered into their labours.

[39]And many of the Samaritans of that city believed on him for the saying of the woman, which testified, He told me all that ever I did. [40]So when the Samaritans were come unto him, they besought him that he would tarry with them: and he abode there two days. [41]And many more believed because of his own word; [42]And said unto the woman, Now we believe, not because of thy saying: for we have heard him ourselves, and know that this is indeed the Christ, the Saviour of the world.

I Am He

In the Bible there is a certain Person who was promised to appear within the history of one nation, a nation that worshiped this Person. They believed the promise that this great Person would come and they continued to worship Him from generation to generation. Then, one day, Someone appeared and said, "I am He." In that case, what do you think would happen? Would the various methods of worship be needed any more? They would no longer be necessary.

The Samaritan woman said to Jesus, "It has always been our tradition to worship on this mountain, Mount Gerizim, but Your people, the Jews, say that it is in Jerusalem that men should worship. Which is correct?" To this Jesus replied:

> "The hour cometh, when ye shall neither in this mountain, nor yet at Jerusalem, worship the Father. Ye worship ye know not what: we know what we worship: for salvation is of the Jews." John 4:21-22

The Jews and the Samaritans worshiped God, but Jesus said they were both wrong; this was not the way to do it. Then He explained the true way to worship God.

The woman said, "I know that Messias cometh, which is called Christ: when he is come, he will tell us all things." To this Jesus replied, "I that speak unto thee am he." The woman's face must have become flushed at the great shock of hearing these words. She came to realize that this Man standing before her was the Messiah.

This was a tremendous event. It was a turning point in this woman's life. She had come to the well to draw water because she was thirsty, but she had not even filled her waterpot; she had been carrying on a continuous conversation. As she talked with Jesus, she asked Him to give her eternal living water so that she would not have to come to the well and draw water again. When Jesus told her that He was the Messiah, she even left her waterpot by the well as she ran back into the city.

Let's think about the change that came about in this woman's heart. It must have been tremendous. If, as Jesus spoke with the woman, He had said to her, "It would be a shame if I only spoke with you, go back into the city and bring your neighbors, too," would she have done as He said? If He had said this, it would have been a great burden for her; she would have become even thirstier. Once this transformation came over her heart, however, she even forgot about her thirst and she ran back to the city of her own accord.

Such is the change that comes about the spirit of an individual when he is born again in the course of his life in this world. It was the change that had come over this woman's spirit that drove her to run back to the city. The desire arose within her to tell others about what she had received. It was not that she expected to gain anything in return for doing this; she was simply reacting to something she had already received. This is what arose from the conversation between Jesus and this woman.

A Mighty Fortress Is Our God

The same goes for us. As we live in this world, what is it that most takes hold of our spirits? What do our hearts pursue? Where do our interests lie? What has filled up our thoughts until now? Perhaps you know the hymn that includes these words:

> Ah! Soul, are you here without comfort or rest,
> Marching down the rough pathway of time?
> Make Jesus your Friend 'ere the shadows grow dark,
> Oh, accept this sweet peace so sublime.[1]

From time to time, when I come up against difficulties, I think about how the Christians who have gone before us faced their struggles.

Long ago in a certain country, there was a man who was facing condemnation. It was a country in which the religious leaders were extremely powerful, and they denounced this man as a traitor. He was a priest who had been ordained to live in absolute compliance with the dictates of a certain enormous church, but one day he came to experience true faith and began to advocate this faith. Consequently, he was summoned before the diet of the Holy Roman Empire at Worms where it seemed he would almost certainly be condemned to death—no one who appeared before that court survived. Do you know who this man was? It was Martin Luther.

Amongst Luther's admirers were some knights who were also skilled swordsmen and they offered to protect him should his life be endangered. Luther did not accept their offer, however, and neither did he put his trust in them. He said that he did not need their protection and that he would go together with his Lord. "Even if the devil were to bring an army against me as great in number as the tiles on the roof of the Diet Building in Worms, I will have the Lord on my side." Such was his resolve. He was the person who wrote the following hymn:

> A mighty Fortress is our God,
> A Bulwark never failing.[2]

This man had found the One in whom he could trust and upon whom he could depend. "My Lord is a mighty Fortress." A fortress acts as a shield to ward off any arrows that may come flying. In his hymn, Luther wrote of the kind of faith that can deal with any problem that may come along.

You may boast that you are healthy and that you can endure the cold very well, but what would happen if you were to take off your clothes and go outside in the middle of winter? You would soon be shivering with cold and wishing you had some warm clothes to put on, or that you could at least get into your car, wouldn't you? In any case, you would need to go inside somewhere where the temperature was more suitable to your needs. You would not be able to overcome the cold by your own strength. It is the same for the faith of each of us individually. Once we have come to believe in Jesus Christ, we need to live with the Bible close at hand. We will not be able to cope if we do not live in this way.

The Samaritan woman who appears in this passage is a shadow of us. She is our predecessor, and we are in the same position as she was. How have we lived our lives? We have tried everything we can think of in the world to fill the emptiness inside us, but nothing has satisfied us. Isn't this why we experience so much distress? Don't all these things only bring conflict to our spirits? This Samaritan woman experienced Jesus' words firsthand and a new light shone in her spirit.

"Sir, I perceive that thou art a prophet." John 4:19

Here the woman had a breakthrough.

The Hour Cometh, When Ye shall Worship the Father

Whenever this woman faced a difficult problem in the course of her life, was troubled in her spirit, or thought about what would happen to her after she died, she would always go to Mount Gerizim in Samaria to worship. Now, however, as she met and spoke with Jesus, she experienced a real inner conflict and spiritual distress. This problem needed to be solved, but she could not just leave Jesus and go to the mountain. So before making a move, she first asked Jesus which was the correct mountain on which they should worship.

> "Our fathers worshipped in this mountain; and ye say, that in Jerusalem is the place where men ought to worship." John 4:20

The matter as to where this woman was supposed to worship needed to be settled in her heart once and for all. You have probably had a similar experience. What is the first thing people do when they come up against difficulties? Even people who do not observe any particular religion will often be heard to use the expression, "Oh, my God." This is one kind of manifestation of a religious mentality. Some people seek out a church when they come up against difficulties. They turn to worshiping God when they encounter suffering. In some countries, when there is a drought, for example, people offer sacrifices in the mountains. They beat drums, make fires, and create quite a commotion as they pray for rain.

Here we might consider why it is that religions have come into being throughout the human race. Why has this happened? When people's consciences are troubling them or they are suffering, the first thing they turn to is religion. They look for a place to worship. This woman, too, was searching for an object of worship, and so she began to ask Jesus. One method that people use to try to escape from the pangs of their conscience is by worshiping someone or something. In movies sometimes there are scenes in which a killer shoots someone and then makes a sign of the cross. There are also many people who use the expression, "Oh Lord!" Many religions start out this way.

What is at the core of man's spirit? Within man's spirit there is a longing for religion. In his heart, man yearns for eternity. This is why people turn to some form of ritual worship when they are in distress. Man has a natural tendency toward religion.

This woman asked whether Jerusalem was the place for religious worship, as advocated by the Jews, or whether the correct place was the local mountain, as the Samaritans claimed. But Jesus answered her on an entirely different level.

> "Jesus saith unto her, Woman, believe me, the hour cometh, when ye shall neither in this mountain, nor yet at Jerusalem, worship the Father."
>
> John 4:21

Jesus told her that the place of worship of the Samaritans was not correct and neither was that of the Jews. He cancelled out all the existing places of worship. He was saying that both those who worshiped on Mount Gerizim and those who worshiped in Jerusalem were wrong. The woman was probably stunned by this response. She had thought this Man was a Jew, but here He was telling her not to worship in Jerusalem either.

"The Father" here is the One to whom Jesus alone could refer in this way with certainty. God was not anyone else's Father, was He? He was there with them, as Jesus and this woman conversed, and so Jesus said, "Believe me."

This was the first time that such an event had occurred along the path that mankind had been walking. The Old Testament, which had taken more than 1400 years to record, was now complete, and it was time for the New Testament to be started. It was time for the beginning of the new promise, and this new promise was now being directly and firmly imprinted in this woman's heart. This was when God was there with them. So Jesus said, "The hour cometh, when ye shall … worship the Father."

Ye Shall Worship the Father in Spirit and in Truth

> "Ye worship ye know not what: we know what we worship: for salvation is of the Jews." John 4:22

"Ye" here does not only apply to the Samaritans; all of the Jews are included. None of them knew what it meant to truly worship God. There was enmity between the Jews and the Samaritans even as they both worshiped God, but in God's eyes they were all in the position of this woman who had sinned. When Jesus said, "Woman," here, He was, of course, addressing the Samaritan woman, but these words were actually meant for all the Samaritans and Jews.

In that case, who does "we" refer to here? It refers to God who said, "Beside me there is no saviour." God the Father, God the Son, and God the Holy Spirit are all one. Since Jesus was God who came in the body of a man, He said, "The hour cometh, when ye shall … worship the Father," and then went on to say, "We know what we worship." This "we" does not include any of the Jews at all. No person, no matter who he or she may be, can be included in this "we." Only God knows what true worship is. Jesus was speaking here not as a Jew, but as God. It is only when we learn the things Jesus referred to as "that we do know," that we are able to worship God in spirit and in truth. Also, in John chapter 3 verse 11 Jesus said, "We speak that we do know, and testify that we have seen." Here again, "we" is used in reference to God as a trinity.

When Jesus said, "Salvation is of the Jews," it means that God's promise was contained within the history of the Jews, as were God's glory and the methods of worship, and it was from among the Jews that the object of their worship, the Christ, was to be born. That is not to say that the Jews made up the concept of salvation. Jesus was born amongst the Israelites and completed the way of salvation. It is this Jesus that we worship.

The woman lived in a state of thirst; she was ready to burst with resentment. Just imagine the torment she must have felt as everything she did created a problem for the neighborhood women who picked on her constantly. Living in such a village left her spirit parched and her throat dry, so she needed to draw some water. The other women in the village would have gone out together with their waterpots to the well, chattering as they went, but this woman crept out by herself in the heat of the day to draw some water. When she got there, to her surprise, she found a man, a Jew, sitting there by the well. In the course of this encounter, the woman heard some words that left her completely at a loss:

"Go, call your husband, and come here."

At these words, the walls around this woman's heart came crashing down. What happened to her in the end? This woman had come with her waterpot to draw water from the well, but now she left the waterpot behind and went back into the city.

Jesus' disciples had gone to buy food in the city from which this woman came. What, then, is the difference between the woman and the disciples? There was no difference between the woman who was thirsty and went out to the well to draw some water and the disciples who were hungry and went to buy some food. That is to say, the Samaritan woman and the Jews were in the same position. They were the same; Jesus alone was different. He did not receive and drink any water from the Samaritan woman, and neither did He eat the food that His disciples brought back. When the disciples urged Him to eat, He said something very strange and completely unexpected:

"I have meat to eat that ye know not of." John 4:32

What in the world did this mean? This was an event in which the life of man, existing within the confines of time, came in touch with

God, who dwells in eternity. It was a matter of Jesus, the Son of God, coming in direct contact with all the descendants of Adam, who are born on this earth.

> "But the hour cometh, and now is, when the true worshippers shall worship the Father in spirit and in truth: for the Father seeketh such to worship him." John 4:23

"The true worshippers shall worship the Father in spirit and in truth." Worshiping in spirit and in truth does not mean putting all your efforts into attending services of worship and remaining faithful to the end, come rain or snow. It does not mean leading a good religious life; offering donations to church despite personal financial difficulties; or engaging in concentrated prayer for everyone and everything in the world. This is a matter that lies on a completely different plane. It demands a tremendous effort to have the patience for Zen-Buddhist meditation, but the roots of Christianity are so firmly embedded that even if you could combine all the efforts devoted to all the different religions and applied them to your prayers, this too, in itself, would not amount to true worship. Neither does it involve the application of the sort of strength or courage that wells up from inside of man such as the determined perseverance and strength with which Jacob wrestled with the angel.

When Jesus said here, "The hour cometh … when the true worshippers shall worship the Father in spirit and in truth," it means that the Holy Spirit of God would come in search of those who are able to submit quietly before God. This does not mean that such people already exist, and God is looking for them as though playing a game of hide and seek. Jesus said that such an hour was coming. When is this hour? It is the moment when the individual discovers that Jesus truly is the Savior.

Jesus was announcing here that through the guidance of the Holy Spirit, people would begin to worship God in spirit. There is no need here for any of man's efforts or strength. There is an issue that we need to understand deeply as we read the Bible. It is a matter that can easily be misunderstood. Worshiping in spirit and in truth does not involve any kind of resolve in our hearts, and neither does it involve relying on any inner strength of our own. Who is it that is to be worshiped in spirit and in truth? It is Jesus. Let's turn now to Romans chapter 9.

> "I say the truth in Christ, I lie not, my conscience also bearing me witness in the Holy Ghost, That I have great heaviness and continual sorrow in my heart. For I could wish that myself were accursed from Christ for my brethren, my kinsmen according to the flesh: Who are Israelites; to whom pertaineth the adoption, and the glory, and the covenants, and the giving of the law, and the service of God, and the promises; Whose are the fathers, and of whom as concerning the flesh Christ came, who is over all, God blessed for ever. Amen."
>
> Romans 9:1-5

As Paul wrote, the Jews had the covenants, the law, the service of God, and the promises. Even so, they rejected Jesus Christ. This is because they did not know the object of their worship. In this passage it says, "Of whom as concerning the flesh Christ came." Christ was born amongst the Jews, as Jesus also said, "Salvation is of the Jews." This was the One "who is over all, God blessed for ever."

In view of all this, where can we offer true worship? The Jews built a magnificent temple where they worshiped and offered sacrifices, and yet the One who said, "Heaven is my throne, and earth is my footstool: what house will ye build me? ... or what is the place of my rest?" Acts 7:49, was Jesus who is the true temple. The only place where we can truly worship God is in Jesus.

> "God is a Spirit: and they that worship him must worship him in spirit and in truth."
>
> John 4:24

"God is a Spirit." The Father of spirits is worshiped in spirit and in truth when the Holy Spirit comes to the spirit of an individual. It is through the Holy Spirit that we worship before God.

I that Speak unto Thee Am He

"The woman saith unto him, I know that Messias cometh, which is called Christ: when he is come, he will tell us all things." John 4:25

The woman said that when the Messiah came, He would declare all things, even to her people, the Samaritans. How did Jesus respond to this?

"Jesus saith unto her, I that speak unto thee am he." John 4:26

These are not words that just anyone can hear and accept. Even in the case of a person who knows and has heard a great deal about Jesus, it is only when his spiritual problems have been solved through the Bible that he is able to say, "Oh, He was my Savior! He has saved me! That's the answer!" Such is the expression of a heart just like that of the Samaritan woman as she heard the words, "I that speak unto thee am he." Such is a heart that has come to know Jesus.

Who said, "I that speak unto thee am he"?

Zacchaeus also had a similar experience. He exerted himself and climbed a sycamore tree to try to see Jesus, but Jesus had already seen him. When Jesus said, "Zacchaeus, make haste, and come down," their eyes met, and a new change came about in Zacchaeus' heart.

If I were to express this in a picture, I would draw a silkworm creeping along a sycamore branch to eat one of the leaves and I would call him, "Mr. Zacchaeus." It seems Zacchaeus was a very short man. He wanted to see Jesus' face, but was not tall enough even to catch a glimpse of Him as he stood in the midst of the large crowd. Like Zacchaeus, who was small in stature, we are all lacking in some way. So we have no choice but to rely on something to make our way up to God.

Zacchaeus climbed a sycamore tree so that he could look down and see Jesus, but Jesus had already seen him and He spoke first, calling up to him, "Zacchaeus, make haste, and come down; for today I must abide at thy house." Just as Jesus came along and told Zacchaeus to come down, He is also first to speak to us, telling us to put aside our arrogant hearts and all our laborious efforts and look once more to Him. Zacchaeus was so grateful that he said, "Behold, Lord, the half of my goods I give to the poor; and if I have taken anything from any man by false accusation, I restore him fourfold" Luke 19:8. Once the true light shone into Zacchaeus' heart, the darkness fled like an insect when it scuttles from the light. Such was Zacchaeus' experience.

"Jesus saith unto her, I that speak unto thee am he." John 4:26

A change takes place in your heart when you personally come to believe in Jesus; when you come to know how the cross of Jesus is related to you; when you realize that it was for your sins that Jesus was crucified and that your sins have been forgiven through the blood of Jesus Christ; when you come to know that He was resurrected and He lives as Mediator between you and God.

"Lord! I believe. I accept You. From this moment, I will live as Your child."

Here the words, "I that speak unto thee," are addressed to each of us individually. When you come to know that Jesus died to atone for your sins, just as was foretold in all the prophecies in the Old Testament regarding the Christ, you know that Jesus was speaking to you personally when He said, "I that speak unto thee am he." Perhaps you are familiar with the following hymn:

> My burden fell off at the pierced feet
> Of the Stranger of Galilee

> And I felt I could love Him forever,
> So gracious and tender was He!
> I claimed Him that day as my Savior,
> This Stranger of Galilee.[3]

What magnificent words! "I that speak to thee am he." If these words were not there for us throughout our lives, there would be no hope for us.

> My hope is built on nothing less
> Than Jesus' blood and righteousness;
> I dare not trust the sweetest frame,
> But wholly lean on Jesus' name.
>
> On Christ, the solid Rock, I stand;
> All other ground is sinking sand,
> All other ground is sinking sand.[4]

"On Christ, the solid Rock, I stand." The Samaritan woman stood upon the words of Jesus Christ.

> "In the beginning was the Word, and the Word was with God, and the Word was God. ... And the Word was made flesh, and dwelt among us, (and we beheld his glory, the glory as of the only begotten of the Father,) full of grace and truth." John 1:1, 14

The Word made flesh came to this world. My spirit stands firm on the word of God. This is what the Samaritan woman experienced the moment Jesus said, "I that speak unto thee am he."

Come and See! Is This Not the Christ?

> "And upon this came his disciples, and marvelled that he talked with the woman: yet no man said, What seekest thou? or, Why talkest thou with her?" John 4:27

None of the disciples asked Jesus why He was speaking with this woman. Why would this be? It seems that the disciples felt uncomfortable when they saw their Teacher, whom they trusted and followed, sitting in conversation with a Samaritan woman, a person that the Jews would have treated as being less than human. Let's try to imagine this scene. It says that the disciples did not even ask Jesus what He was talking about with the woman. They probably all simply exchanged glances. When they came back with the food they had bought and found Jesus and the woman, they were speechless and probably agreed amongst themselves not to say anything.

> "The woman then left her waterpot, and went her way into the city, and saith to the men." John 4:28

The woman did not even fill her waterpot; she left it empty by the well and returned to the city. She had had a clear purpose in coming to the well, hadn't she? She had intended to fill her waterpot and take it home. When she got to the well, however, she met a Man she did not expect to see and she did not get around to drawing any water. As she spoke with the Man, her heart became filled with a fountain of water. So she went, leaving her empty waterpot behind. What happened to the waterpot after that is anyone's guess; she just left it there. Similar verses to this appear in other parts of the Bible.

> "And Jesus said unto him, No man, having put his hand to the plough, and looking back, is fit for the kingdom of God." Luke 9:62

The woman put aside any notion that she herself might in any human way be able to solve the problems in her life or the conflict in her heart, and then she returned to her city.

She and the disciples entered the same city, but there was a huge difference between when she now went back there and when the disciples went there to buy food. Why was this? They had different purposes. The disciples went to make the preparations to fill their stomachs, but Jesus had already filled this woman's spirit.

So the woman ran back to the city because her spirit had been filled without her having to fill her waterpot. In the city, she shouted out to gather together all the people she knew. Since it was lunchtime, some people might even have come running out in the middle of their meal. What did the woman shout out?

> "Come, see a man, which told me all things that ever I did: is not this the Christ?" John 4:29

The woman returned to the city to evangelize. She went as a missionary. She had come out to the well to quench her physical thirst, but now she went running to quench the thirst in other people's spirits. She began the work that even the disciples had not dared to attempt.

At the wedding in Cana, Mary, the mother of Jesus, had told her Son, "They have no wine," and the waterpots had come to be filled. The Samaritan woman's spiritual thirst was quenched, so she left her waterpot behind and went to tell others to "Come and see." From the very beginning these words, "Come and see," were used continually in evangelizing. You will probably recall how Philip told Nathanael to "Come and see." This is how evangelizing begins. This woman also shouted out, "Come, see a man which told me all things that ever I did: is not this the Christ?" She said this Man knew everything about her.

> "Then they went out of the city, and came unto him." John 4:30

The woman had come to the well earlier to draw water, and now the people of her city came to Jesus, the wellspring of water. This was the moment at which man's life that exists within the temporal realms of this world connected with God who dwells in eternity.

My Food

> "In the mean while his disciples prayed him, saying, Master, eat. But he said unto them, I have meat to eat that ye know not of. Therefore said the disciples one to another, Hath any man brought him ought to eat?"
> John 4:31-33

The disciples took the opportunity to bring Jesus some food and urge Him to eat, and Jesus' response was very simple: "I have meat to eat that ye know not of." When Jesus said this, a question arose in the minds of His disciples. They thought that perhaps He was full because someone had already brought Him some food to eat, but what did Jesus say?

> "Jesus saith unto them, My meat is to do the will of him that sent me, and to finish his work."
> John 4:34

There are many people in this world who are preoccupied with the ordinary matters of everyday life. There are also people who try to ease their tired minds or to calm their troubled hearts by reading books or delving deeply into some subject of study. People who are happy simply eating and drinking cannot understand this. You might hear them saying something like:

"He just studies all day and doesn't even think about eating."

Or:

"All he ever does is read."

When someone eats something and comments, "That was delicious," or "I'm full," or "That's good," his judgment is based simply on the workings of the brain. Quite apart from this kind of physical satisfaction that comes from eating or drinking something good, we often receive slightly more psychological comfort from reading a book or a poem, or singing a song. There have probably been times, even when you were a child, when you have been so engrossed in a book that you have forgotten to eat. Your mind gets completely absorbed in your book.

How about Jesus? Aside from filling His stomach, every step He took on this earth, every word He spoke, and each and every one of His actions had to fulfill the prophecies in the Old Testament. While Jesus was completing His time on this earth, God's word was continually being fulfilled in His body.

> "I have meat to eat that ye know not of. … My meat is to do the will of him that sent me, and to finish his work." John 4:32, 34

> "And he said unto them, These are the words which I spake unto you, while I was yet with you, that all things must be fulfilled, which were written in the law of Moses, and in the prophets, and in the psalms, concerning me." Luke 24:44

Jesus knew that the prophecies recorded in the Scriptures were being fulfilled in Him. At this time, He was unaware of His physical thirst and had forgotten all about His hunger. This has probably happened to you as well on occasions. After I had come to realize God's love and come to know His grace, I began to evangelize. At such times, if I was talking about the Bible and someone came and set a table of food in front of me, urging me to eat, it would seem to me that that person was trying to interfere with the furtherance of the gospel, and I would become irritated. I would think to myself, "But this is so much more urgent." I was more eager to bring other people to realize the truth of the gospel—since this was my duty.

> O happy day, that fixed my choice
> On Thee my Saviour and my God!
> Well may this glowing heart rejoice,
> And tell its raptures all abroad.

> Happy day, happy day,
> When Jesus washed my sins away.
> He taught me how to watch and pray;
> And live rejoicing ev'ry day.
> Happy day, happy day,
> When Jesus washed my sins away.
>
> 'Tis done, the great transaction's done;
> I am my Lord's and He is mine.
> He drew me, and I followed on,
> Charmed to confess the Voice divine.[5]

It was precisely this work that had started to be accomplished here.

"I have meat to eat that ye know not of. … My meat is to do the will of him that sent me, and to finish his work."

As you walk step by step with Jesus and in the end see Him nailed to the cross, you come to realize that Jesus has taken all of your suffering and your entire burden upon Himself. Jesus' words were a promise to bear the whole of our burden. He said that His food was to proclaim the words of the gospel continually to mankind.

Jesus came to teach us that the ordinary matters of everyday life are not man's ultimate purpose and that God's aim is to save the spirits of men. Here He said that His food was to do the will of His Father and finish His work. In the end, when He had completed this work, He said, "It is finished," didn't He? Until that time, until Jesus completely accomplished the will of His Father on the cross, He was fulfilling, in His body, all the words of the Scriptures.

Later the apostle Paul said:

> "[I] fill up that which is behind of the afflictions of Christ in my flesh for his body's sake, which is the church."   Colossians 1:24

Paul said that he was filling up in his own flesh the remainder of the sufferings of Jesus.

White Already to Harvest

> "Say not ye, There are yet four months, and then cometh harvest? behold, I say unto you, Lift up your eyes, and look on the fields; for they are white already to harvest." John 4:35

"Lift up your eyes and look at the fields. The grain is already ripe. The ears of corn are white and hanging down under the weight of the grain." When grains ripen, they lose their green color, don't they? Jesus was saying, "The fields have changed color. You think that there are still four months to the harvest. But I tell you the crops are already ripe and ready to be harvested." What are the crops that He was talking about?

> "And he that reapeth receiveth wages, and gathereth fruit unto life eternal: that both he that soweth and he that reapeth may rejoice together. And herein is that saying true, One soweth, and another reapeth." John 4:36-37

"You think that there are still four months until the harvest." In the eyes of Jesus, the fields were already white for harvest. Whose eyes do you think saw correctly? When Jesus said, "Lift up your eyes, and look on the fields," He was not talking about the crops that would not be ready for harvest until four months later—the crops that would satisfy the physical hunger of the people of this world. It would be four months before those crops would be ready for harvest, just as the disciples thought. It was the matter of food made from crops such as these that was the subject of conversation amongst the disciples when they said, "Hath any man brought him ought to eat?" At that time, Jesus told them that He had a different kind of food.

By this time the Samaritan woman had already begun the work of a missionary as she ran into the city and brought the people there to Jesus. Only a few days earlier, these people had been cold-hearted towards this woman and treated her with contempt, but now they followed her. Perhaps they had seen her through their windows as she had gone out to draw water, but now she came running back, leaving her waterpot behind. It must have seemed to them that there might be something in what she said, and so they followed her out to the well.

There was something that Jesus needed to do for the people who came with the Samaritan woman. Earlier He had promised to give the woman eternal living water and had quenched her thirsty spirit. Similarly, now that these people had followed the woman, curious to know what was going on, there was something that Jesus needed to do for them.

That is why Jesus, who had not yet eaten anything, spoke in this way to His disciples when they brought some food. As they were discussing whether or not someone had already brought Him something to eat, He said:

"It is another four months until harvest time, but lift up your eyes and look at the fields. The time to harvest is already here."

Why did He tell them to lift up their eyes? They did not need to look up, did they? They could have looked down and still seen the whole field of grain. Here, when Jesus said, "Lift up your eyes, and look on the fields," He was not talking about food for the body. On another occasion, Jesus said, "Labour not for the meat which perisheth, but for that meat which endureth unto everlasting life" John 6:27. In a similar vein, Jesus was telling His disciples here to look at the people the woman had run to fetch and all the other people gathered in the society in which they had been to buy bread, people they could understand and with whom they could communicate. The spirits of these people were already full of grain and ready for harvest. The judgment had begun for their spirits and the deciding factor was whether or not they believed. Jesus was saying that the spirits of others need to be saved.

> "Say not ye, There are yet four months, and then cometh harvest? behold, I say unto you, Lift up your eyes, and look on the fields; for they are white already to harvest." John 4:35

When I am walking along by the fields and I see the golden ears of corn bent over with the heavy weight of the grain they hold, it reminds me of a hymn:

> Far and near the fields are teeming
> With the waves of ripened grain;
> Far and near their gold is gleaming,
> O'er the sunny slope and plain.[6]

These ears of corn are full of spiritual struggles. Jesus was speaking of His desire for this grain to be harvested quickly.

> When the harvest is completed
> And the last grain safely stor'd,
> Then with joy shall we be seated
> At the banquet of the Lord.
> Lord of harvest, send forth reapers!
> Hear us, Lord to Thee we cry;
> Send them now the sheaves to gather,
> Ere the harvest time pass by.[7]

Jesus was explaining to His disciples that the spirits of these people could be harvested with just a slight touch of the sickle.

> "I sent you to reap that whereon ye bestowed no labour: other men laboured." John 4:38

"Other men laboured, and ye are entered into their labours." Who are these "other men"?

> Hail to the brightness of Zion's glad morning!
> Long by the prophets of Israel foretold!
> Hail to the millions from bondage returning!
> Gentiles and Jews the blest vision behold.[8]

The gospel announced by the prophets in the Psalms and the Old Testament writings of Moses and the prophets were later to be accompanied by the New Testament writings of the apostles. Thus the apostles joined in to complete the work proclaimed by the prophets. This is why Jesus said, "Other men laboured, and ye are entered into their labours."

Many of the Samaritans Believed on Him

> "And many of the Samaritans of that city believed on him for the saying of the woman, which testified, He told me all that ever I did."
> John 4:39

When the woman explained to the people in the city how Jesus had told her everything she had ever done in the past, many of them believed. It says, "Many of the Samaritans of that city believed on him."

> "So when the Samaritans were come unto him, they besought him that he would tarry with them: and he abode there two days."
> John 4:40

The Samaritans were a people scorned by the Jews. Nevertheless, when the Samaritans came to Jesus and asked Him to stay with them, He stayed there for two days. In doing this, He was acting in a manner completely free from all Jewish tradition, the Jewish sense of superiority over the Samaritans, and the hatred and scorn that the

Jews generally felt towards these people. Jesus' disciples thought it strange that He should even converse with this Samaritan woman, didn't they? They were simply left speechless. But for Him to actually stay with the Samaritans for two days was a matter without precedent. How long did He stay there in terms of hours? He was there for the long period of forty-eight hours. Many people are born and die within such a period of time.

Even though many people in Jerusalem had believed in Jesus, and there were many people who had followed Him from Galilee, the Bible says that He did not entrust Himself to them.

> "Now when he was in Jerusalem at the passover, in the feast day, many believed in his name, when they saw the miracles which he did. But Jesus did not commit himself unto them, because he knew all men." John 2:23-24

Jerusalem was a city that prided itself on its religious orthodoxy. It was a place where the words of the law and all the prophets were accepted and many of the people living there considered themselves to be righteous. Nevertheless, Jesus did not entrust Himself to anyone there.

What is the significance of Jesus staying with the people in this city in Samaria? It can be associated with the fact that He humbled Himself and obeyed even to death. In the eyes of the Jewish priests and religious leaders, Jesus behaved in a manner that rendered Him worthy of death. Since the Samaritans were a forsaken people, Jesus was inclined all the more to spend these two days with them.

> "And many more believed because of his own word." John 4:41

Earlier we read that many people believed because of what the woman had said, but then many more came to believe because of the words they heard directly from Jesus when they came to meet Him in person.

We Know that This Is Indeed the Savior of the World

> "And said unto the woman, Now we believe, not because of thy saying: for we have heard him ourselves, and know that this is indeed the Christ, the Saviour of the world." John 4:42

"We have heard Him ourselves." What kind of Savior did they now know Him to be? He is the Savior of the world. They had thought that the Messiah was to be the Savior of the Jews alone. They had thought that salvation was only for the Jews, but the Samaritans also came to realize that Jesus was the Savior of the world, the One who brought salvation to the whole world.

Let's think about this for a moment: what is the situation in your household? Is there anyone in your family who might say, "How can you expect me to believe in Jesus when I see the way you behave?" Is there anyone in your family who turns you down flatly with a firm, "No, thank you," no matter how much you urge him or her to believe in Jesus? Most people scrutinize the behavior of family members who evangelize to them. If such people then come to a firm belief in Jesus through reading the Bible and coming to realize the truth in its message, they may be heard to say something similar to the words of these Samaritans:

> "For we have heard him ourselves, and know that this is indeed the Christ, the Saviour of the world." John 4:42

Thus we can see that there is a difference between hearing the message proclaimed by this woman and hearing the words of the Bible directly from Jesus. The woman proclaimed the message, but more people believed when they heard Jesus' words directly.

> "And said unto the woman, Now we believe, not because of thy saying." John 4:42

"It is not because you are such a good speaker."

"For we have heard him ourselves, and know that this is indeed the Christ, the Saviour of the world."

The woman had run back to the city and done her best to explain. Just as the Samaritan woman had heard the voice of Jesus, saying, "I that speak unto thee am he," these Samaritans also heard Jesus for themselves and believed.

When we come to know the love of God and see that other people are troubled in their spirits, we feel we want to tell them about the gospel so we open our Bibles and begin to explain. There are many people, however, who fail in this work because they make a great effort to go about it in their own way. When we are spreading the gospel to others, we must treat the Bible as something truly precious. This is because the words recorded in the Bible are so very precious. That is not to say that we should idolize the Bible. Since the Bible contains the words of God, when we are explaining the gospel to others, we need to do it seriously, taking even greater care than we might if we were dealing with a chest filled with precious stones. If we do this, one by one, others will begin to come to Jesus and understand why they have been urged to believe.

Spiritual Service of Worship

There was a man who was traveling around arresting and killing anyone who believed in Jesus when suddenly he came up against a wall of darkness. This man was Saul who came to be called Paul. He heard a voice calling out to him:

"Saul, Saul."

And this man who had known nothing but the law asked:

"Who art thou, Lord?"

"I am Jesus whom thou persecutest."

When Paul heard this, he fell to the ground.[9] Later Paul spoke with great sincerity about worshiping before God:

> "I beseech you therefore, brethren, by the mercies of God, that ye present your bodies a living sacrifice, holy, acceptable unto God, which is your reasonable service." Romans 12:1

Jesus said, "But the hour cometh ... when the true worshippers shall worship the Father in spirit and in truth." And He said that "the Father seeketh such to worship him." And then Paul wrote, "Present your bodies a living sacrifice, holy, acceptable unto God." This happens when our spirits are used in the work of spreading the gospel to others.

> "That I should be the minister of Jesus Christ to the Gentiles, ministering the gospel of God, that the offering up of the Gentiles might be acceptable, being sanctified by the Holy Ghost." Romans 15:16

Paul said that he offered the Gentiles up to God. He led Gentiles to salvation and presented them as a sacrificial offering before God. Paul's attitude as he lived his life was just like the way this woman acted here.

This woman was overjoyed when she heard Jesus say, "But the hour cometh ... when the true worshippers shall worship ... in spirit and in truth," and "I that speak unto thee am he." She left her waterpot behind and ran off to spread the gospel to others. She explained the gospel to the people of her city and brought them to hear Jesus' words for themselves. In the meantime, Jesus had been teaching His disciples. As the woman was speaking to the people who gathered round her, telling them about the Christ, Jesus was teaching His disciples the importance of evangelizing. He was telling them about the willingness to offer one's body as a living sacrifice—about true spiritual worship.

The worship about which the apostle Paul spoke is the responsibility held by those who have already realized the truth of the gospel, the responsibility they have for the spirits of others as they live their lives on this earth, their duty to bring others to salvation. The accomplishing of this duty is what God truly desires.

When We Worship in Spirit and in Truth

> "But the hour cometh, and now is, when the true worshippers shall worship the Father in spirit and in truth: for the Father seeketh such to worship him." John 4:23

Who are the people who fulfill God's desire and complete the work that He wants carried out? They are the Christians who proclaim the gospel. Jesus teaches the believers to be responsible for the spirits of others. The Bible explains that, since God has blotted out our sins for all time, this good news is to be proclaimed to the ends of the earth, in the east and in the west, everywhere, so that this eternal sacrifice, this eternal service or worship, may be offered continually—the sacrifice of people throughout the world believing that Christ is the Savior and accepting the Son of God.

> "For from the rising of the sun even unto the going down of the same my name shall be great among the Gentiles; and in every place incense shall be offered unto my name, and a pure offering: for my name shall be great among the heathen, saith the Lord of hosts." Malachi 1:11

What do these words from Malachi tell us? The Bible says that our spirits are cleansed before God through blood, doesn't it? Since we have been cleansed through blood, we are presented to God as an acceptable offering; in other words, our individual spirits come to praise God.

From long ago, the Israelites went to Jerusalem to worship even when they were scattered and lived among other nations, even when they mingled with other peoples, even when they became of mixed blood and assumed different nationalities. They went to Jerusalem once a year and worshiped there. About two thousand years ago a man from the land of Cush, or Ethiopia, also came to Jerusalem to worship. He was a eunuch in charge of the national treasury under Candace, the queen of Ethiopia. In today's terms, he would have been the equivalent of a minister of finance. Like this eunuch, the Jews continued to gather in Jerusalem in order to worship no matter where they lived.

> "And they, when they had testified and preached the word of the Lord, returned to Jerusalem, and preached the gospel in many villages of the Samaritans. And the angel of the Lord spake unto Philip, saying, Arise, and go toward the south unto the way that goeth down from Jerusalem unto Gaza, which is desert. And he arose and went: and, behold, a man of Ethiopia, an eunuch of great authority under Candace queen of the Ethiopians, who had the charge of all her treasure, and had come to Jerusalem for to worship, was returning, and sitting in his chariot read Esaias the prophet."
>
> Acts 8:25-28

This man was in charge of the queen's treasury in Ethiopia, far away to the south. He had come to Jerusalem to worship and, since he held a powerful position, he was returning to his country in a chariot. As he was traveling along, he happened to be reading Isaiah chapter 53. At that time, the Holy Spirit led Philip to the place where this man was. Philip approached the chariot and asked, "Do you understand what you are reading?" The eunuch replied, "How can I, unless someone guides me?"

So Philip explained in detail what is recorded about Jesus in the book of Isaiah and the eunuch came to believe in Jesus. He believed immediately and was baptized right there and then. In the past, it was necessary to come to Jerusalem from far away, as the eunuch had done, in order to worship, but now it is possible to worship even in the remotest corners of the earth.

Once the work of the gospel had begun, it became possible to worship anywhere on earth, wherever an individual happens to be when he or she meets Jesus, even in a chariot. This is because Jesus Himself is the temple.

> "The hour cometh, when ye shall neither in this mountain, nor yet at Jerusalem, worship the Father. ... But the hour cometh, and now is, when the true worshippers shall worship the Father in spirit and in truth: for the Father seeketh such to worship him. God is a Spirit: and they that worship him must worship him in spirit and in truth."
>
> John 4:21, 23-24

The Father seeks those who worship in this way, and He found one such person, didn't He? Even in a chariot. This is how He finds people to worship Him. The Bible tells us that such work will be carried out even in the remotest places on earth. This is eternal worship before God.

The fact that the eunuch was reading Isaiah chapter 53 is a lesson to us as well. Without any need for analysis, the words written 700 years before Jesus came are a lesson for us even today. Many people have come to realize the truth of the gospel while reading Isaiah chapter 53.

The Father seeks those who will really worship in spirit and truth. Why is He seeking them? The Lord saves the spirits of those who will become such worshippers. The Savior of our spirits is seeking those who will worship Him in spirit and truth. In other words, He is seeking those who will carry out the work of spreading the gospel to the ends of the earth. The Jews gathered to worship in Jerusalem, and the Samaritans in Mount Gerizim, but now the worship of God was to spread further afield. Jesus said, "Ye shall be witnesses unto me both in Jerusalem, and in all Judaea, and in Samaria, and unto the uttermost part of the earth" Acts 1:8. The work of these witnesses will continue until the day when the Lord comes again. The Bible tells us that many people from the east and from the west will offer precisely this kind of worship to God, praising Him forever.

13

The Appropriate Response to Faith

John 4:43-54

The nobleman asked his servants when his son had recovered.
He had begun to recover at the seventh hour.
This is approximately the equivalent of one o'clock in the afternoon.
This was also the time of day
when Jesus would later be suffering on the cross.
It was on the strength of Jesus' crucifixion, His suffering, and His death
that He told this man that his son was healed.

John 4:43-54

[43]Now after two days he departed thence, and went into Galilee. [44]For Jesus himself testified, that a prophet hath no honour in his own country. [45]Then when he was come into Galilee, the Galilaeans received him, having seen all the things that he did at Jerusalem at the feast: for they also went unto the feast.

[46]So Jesus came again into Cana of Galilee, where he made the water wine. And there was a certain nobleman, whose son was sick at Capernaum. [47]When he heard that Jesus was come out of Judaea into Galilee, he went unto him, and besought him that he would come down, and heal his son: for he was at the point of death.

[48]Then said Jesus unto him, Except ye see signs and wonders, ye will not believe.

[49]The nobleman saith unto him, Sir, come down ere my child die.

[50]Jesus saith unto him, Go thy way; thy son liveth. And the man believed the word that Jesus had spoken unto him, and he went his way. [51]And as he was now going down, his servants met him, and told him, saying, Thy son liveth. [52]Then inquired he of them the hour when he began to amend. And they said unto him, Yesterday at the seventh hour the fever left him.

[53]So the father knew that it was at the same hour, in the which Jesus said unto him, Thy son liveth: and himself believed, and his whole house. [54]This is again the second miracle that Jesus did, when he was come out of Judaea into Galilee.

The Appropriate Response to Faith

A Prophet Hath No Honor in His Own Country

Now Jesus left the region of Samaria and went to Galilee.

"Now after two days he departed thence, and went into Galilee. For Jesus himself testified, that a prophet hath no honour in his own country." John 4:43-44

"A prophet hath no honour in his own country." Here Jesus meant that the Galileans—His own family and neighbors—disregarded Him. This comes across clearly in all four of the Gospels.

"And when he was come into his own country, he taught them in their synagogue, insomuch that they were astonished, and said, Whence hath this man this wisdom, and these mighty works? Is not this the carpenter's son? is not his mother called Mary? and His brethren, James, and Joses, and Simon, and Judas? And his sisters, are they not all with us? Whence then hath this man all these things? And they were offended in him. But Jesus said unto them, A prophet is not without honour, save in his own country, and in his own house." Matthew 13:54-57

Jesus was treated with utter contempt by the people of His hometown. Even though He did nothing with which they could find fault, they snubbed Him, making comments such as, "Where did this Man get His wisdom and such powers? How did He become so clever? We all know His family." These people did not welcome His presence.

"And the multitude cometh together again, so that they could not so much as eat bread. And when his friends heard of it, they went out to lay hold on him: for they said, He is beside himself." Mark 3:20-21

They said that Jesus was crazy. They thought He should be sawing wood and planing it smooth. Who did He think He was, preaching like that? Now let's take a look at Luke chapter 4 verse 24.

173

"And he said, Verily I say unto you, No prophet is accepted in his own country."

These are the same words that we found Jesus saying in John chapter 4 when He went to Galilee.

The Galileans Received Him

"Then when he was come into Galilee, the Galilaeans received him, having seen all the things that he did at Jerusalem at the feast: for they also went unto the feast." John 4:45

When it says here that the Galileans received Him, it does not mean that they believed He was the Christ or they received Him as the Son of God. They had seen what He had done in Jerusalem and so they received Him into their towns. Jesus was not made welcome in His hometown; He was snubbed and even His own relatives said He was crazy.

What is the significance of all these incidents that Jesus encountered in Galilee and Jerusalem? They are associated with Jesus' crucifixion that lay ahead in Jerusalem. They serve as a reminder that, even though Jesus came according to the prophecies made long before, the Jews had Him put to death. Jerusalem was the place in which Jesus had to suffer and die, but in Galilee too it was clear that He was on His way to His death. The cold reception and scornful treatment He received in Galilee and Jerusalem was a shadow of the death that He would ultimately face in Jerusalem. It was with this in mind that Jesus said, "A prophet hath no honour in his own country." He was not commenting on the character of the Galileans. He was not alluding to a matter of the flesh, but of the soul and the spirit.

In the book of Isaiah it says that even though the people of Galilee walked in darkness, a great light has shone on them.

Even in Galilee, Jesus became Savior to those who received Him as the Christ.

> "Nevertheless the dimness shall not be such as was in her vexation, when at the first he lightly afflicted the land of Zebulun and the land of Naphtali, and afterward did more grievously afflict her by the way of the sea, beyond Jordan, in Galilee of the nations. The people that walked in darkness have seen a great light: they that dwell in the land of the shadow of death, upon them hath the light shined."
> Isaiah 9:1-2

Who was this light? Even in the land of Galilee, He was the Savior, the Messiah, and the Son of God to those who believe in Him. This was the same for the Samaritans, too. Even within these people who treated Him with such disdain, Jesus planted the faith to believe that He was the Christ. Also, it was because they believed in the Savior that prophecies like the verse that we have just read came to be fulfilled.

Awake, O Zion

The same was true in Jerusalem; on the day Jesus was crucified, there were people who came to believe in Him, saying, "Certainly this was a righteous man." Let's turn now to a passage about Jerusalem.

> "Awake, awake; put on thy strength, O Zion; put on thy beautiful garments, O Jerusalem, the holy city: for henceforth there shall no more come into thee the uncircumcised and the unclean. Shake thyself from the dust; arise, and sit down, O Jerusalem: loose thyself from the bands of thy neck, O captive daughter of Zion. For thus saith the Lord, Ye have sold yourselves for nought; and ye shall be redeemed without money."
> Isaiah 52:1-3

These verses prophesied that the people of Jerusalem would be forgiven, and that they would be set free and redeemed without money. We are also told here that the unclean—in other words, those who have sin—will not be able to enter Jerusalem, and then it says, "Arise, and sit down." The God who has promised that He has seated us together with Him in heavenly places has also promised that believers will enter the eternal Jerusalem. This is telling us that we have been set free in Christ.

> Hail to the brightness of Zion's glad morning!
> Long by the prophets of Israel foretold!
> Hail to the millions from bondage returning![1]

This hymn talks of the death that Jesus had to face in Zion—that is to say Jerusalem—the spiritual home of the Jews. Zion was the name of a small hill just outside Jerusalem, but it represents Jerusalem as a whole. In the Bible we read that when the Jews were far away from Jerusalem in a foreign land, they wept when they remembered Zion.

"By the rivers of Babylon, there we sat down, yea, we wept, when we remembered Zion." Psalm 137:1

The Jews sat down by the rivers of Babylon and wept as they longed for Jerusalem.

"How shall we sing the Lord's song in a strange land? If I forget thee, O Jerusalem, let my right hand forget her cunning. If I do not remember thee, let my tongue cleave to the roof of my mouth; if I prefer not Jerusalem above my chief joy." Psalm 137:4-6

Even while they lived as captives in a distant land, the Jews longed for Jerusalem, they prayed for Jerusalem, and they looked toward Jerusalem as they sang God's praises. Such was the heart of the Jews. The prophet Daniel also prayed toward Jerusalem while he was in exile in Babylon.

The Appropriate Response to Faith

> "Now when Daniel knew that the writing was signed, he went into his house; and his windows being open in his chamber toward Jerusalem, he kneeled upon his knees three times a day, and prayed, and gave thanks before his God, as he did aforetime." Daniel 6:10

The Babylonians, who despised Daniel, were aware that he always opened the windows of his room and prayed towards Jerusalem. So they persuaded the king to sign a decree stating that anyone found worshiping any other god than the king within a set period of time was to be put to death. Despite the king's orders, Daniel continued to pray towards Jerusalem. As a result, he was arrested and thrown into the lions' den, but Daniel did not abandon his steadfast faith towards Jerusalem.

Whose Son Was Sick

> "So Jesus came again into Cana of Galilee, where he made the water wine. And there was a certain nobleman, whose son was sick at Capernaum." John 4:46

Jesus came to Cana of Galilee. This was the place where He had performed the astonishing miracle of turning water into wine. News of this incident had spread so that everyone in the neighborhood already knew about it. When Jesus turned the water into wine, His mother had told the servants to do whatever He told them, hadn't she? In the same way, all man has to do is believe what Jesus says.

Here again, faith is revealed by actions. A certain nobleman came looking for Jesus. What kind of man would this have been? As a nobleman, he was probably powerful enough to summon Jesus to him with the simple order of, "Bring Him here to me!" He was a man of great authority. But his son lay sick in Capernaum, a city located about 17 miles from Cana. The nobleman had traveled with all speed this long distance to find Jesus in the hope that his son's life could be spared.

What would a father do today if his child were ill? He would take him to the hospital or call a doctor and arrange the best treatment for the child, wouldn't he? Since this father was a nobleman, he could have ordered that all the doctors in the land be called in. It seems, however, that this son's illness was not easy to cure. No matter what was done for him, the son was not getting any better and now he lay dying. So the nobleman had quickly traveled 17 miles at a single stretch and was now asking Jesus to cure his son. Passages like this in the Bible bring a lump to my throat.

> "When he heard that Jesus was come out of Judaea into Galilee, he went unto him, and besought him that he would come down, and heal his son: for he was at the point of death." John 4:47

He went to Jesus and asked Him to come down to his son. This man of such a high status humbled himself to the utmost as he traveled to the unknown backwater of Cana to implore a man of no apparent position to come and heal his ailing son.

Let's consider what was going on in this man's heart. Those of you who are fathers, shut your eyes and think about this for a minute. When you come up against a problem, do you cling to God to the extent that this man did? It is all too easy to think, "That's what happened in the Bible. I might have done the same thing if I had been in that situation two thousand years ago," but try to imagine a situation like this in your own household today. Consider your attitude when your child is ill, or there is some other problem in your family. Let's take another look at this verse.

> "When he heard that Jesus was come out of Judaea into Galilee, he went unto him, and besought him that he would come down, and heal his son: for he was at the point of death." John 4:47

This man saw that his son was dying and he came to Jesus.

Thy Son Liveth

"Then said Jesus unto him, Except ye see signs and wonders, ye will not believe."
John 4:48

Jesus spoke brusquely as He said, "Except ye see signs and wonders, ye will not believe." Having received this kind of treatment, the nobleman might easily have turned on his heels and gone away, saying, "Do you think you're the only person in the world who can cure the sick? You're nothing but a quack." The man's high position would have warranted this kind of reaction, but he simply stood there pleading.

"The nobleman saith unto him, Sir, come down ere my child die."
John 4:49

Who in this world can we put our hopes in and believe? There is no one but Jesus. This man clung to Jesus having no hope anywhere else. "Sir, come down ere my child die."

"Jesus saith unto him, Go thy way; thy son liveth. And the man believed the word that Jesus had spoken unto him, and he went his way."
John 4:50

Jesus simply said to him, "Go thy way; thy son liveth." The nobleman believed these words and went his way. Let's think about this man's faith. Even though Thomas, who is also called Didymus, traveled around with Jesus for such a long time, what was it that he said later? "Except I shall see in his hands the print of the nails, and put my finger into the print of the nails, and thrust my hand into his side, I will not believe." John 20:25 Then Jesus said to him, "Thomas, because thou hast seen me, thou hast believed: blessed are they that have not seen, and yet have believed" John 20:29.

The nobleman simply believed Jesus' words without actually seeing that his son was healed. In our case, too, as we continue to read the Bible again and again and meditate on its words, our faith is established and matures before God. It is as it says in the Bible, "So then faith cometh by hearing, and hearing by the word of God" Romans 10:17.

> "And as he was now going down, his servants met him, and told him, saying, Thy son liveth. Then inquired he of them the hour when he began to amend. And they said unto him, Yesterday at the seventh hour the fever left him." John 4:51-52

Let's think about this for a moment. This nobleman had hurried to Jesus, heard His words, and was now returning home. It seems that a night had passed. As a nobleman he would have been a very busy man. If he had not believed Jesus' words, he would have hurried straight back to Capernaum to see if his son had indeed been cured without Jesus even seeing him. However, this man simply believed Jesus' words, "Thy son liveth," so he took his time and did not set out for home until the next day. As he was on his way, he met his servants who told him that his son was alive and well.

The nobleman asked his servants when his son had recovered, and they said, "Yesterday at the seventh hour the fever left him." He had begun to recover at the seventh hour. This is approximately the equivalent of one o'clock in the afternoon. This was also the time of day when Jesus would later be suffering on the cross.

> "Surely he hath borne our griefs, and carried our sorrows: yet we did esteem him stricken, smitten of God, and afflicted." Isaiah 53:4

It was on the strength of Jesus' crucifixion, His suffering, and His death that He told this man that his son was healed.

> "But he was wounded for our transgressions, he was bruised for our iniquities: the chastisement of our peace was upon him; and with his stripes we are healed." Isaiah 53:5

This was precisely at the hour of His suffering.

"Who his own self bare our sins in his own body on the tree, that we, being dead to sins, should live unto righteousness: by whose stripes ye were healed. For ye were as sheep going astray; but are now returned unto the Shepherd and Bishop of your souls." 1 Peter 2:24-25

The Bible tells us that when Jesus was whipped and the crown of thorns was forced down onto His brow, at the time of all this suffering, He also bore our griefs and sorrows, taking them upon Himself. The pain and death that should have been ours He took upon Himself.

The son of the nobleman was dying, but Jesus put forward His own death as a guarantee for the child's recovery as He said, "Thy son liveth." He already knew that not long after this, as He hung on the cross and said, "It is finished," He would be carrying upon Himself the sins of all generations. This is why, as the Son of God, He was able to speak these words of promise to the nobleman.

He Himself Believed, and His Whole House

"So the father knew that it was at the same hour, in the which Jesus said unto him, Thy son liveth: and himself believed, and his whole house. This is again the second miracle that Jesus did, when he was come out of Judaea into Galilee." John 4:53-54

This brings to mind another verse from the Bible:

"And they said, Believe on the Lord Jesus Christ, and thou shalt be saved, and thy house.'" Acts 16:31

These are truly words of great blessing! Here we have a promise that if one person of a family truly comes to believe in Jesus, all the rest of the family will also receive salvation. Since we have this promise, we should not spare our words when it comes to spreading the gospel to our families. It may be that they are going through some kind of suffering of which we are unaware, or that when they hear what we are saying, they long to know this truth and later they may come to realize the love of God. If the seed of God's word is sown in their hearts, someday they may be able to come to salvation. It is with faith in this promise that we spread the gospel.

We need to act with faith in God's word. We need to believe what the Bible says and put our trust in these words. Such should be our attitude. This is different from just thinking, "It will probably work out eventually." It is important to put our trust completely in God.

The nobleman's son was ill, but actually we are all ailing to some extent in our hearts. Just as many different illnesses come and go, affecting us physically, there are also illnesses that affect the heart. If someone hurts our pride, for example, we think, "Just you wait!" If someone says something to upset us, inside we boil with rage. Since this is the way we are, shouldn't we put our trust in Jesus? This is why we sing:

> Only trust Him, only trust Him,
> Only trust Him now.[2]

And:

> Faith is the victory! Faith is the victory!
> Oh, glorious victory, that overcomes the world.[3]

It is my hope that we all keep the words of these hymns in our hearts and live by them.

14

The True Sabbath: Eternal Rest

John 5:1-18

When Jesus said that He was the Lord of the Sabbath,
He meant that through the cross,
He filled the deep chasm between man and God.
When man sinned, he broke the Sabbath and therefore
Jesus took this problem upon Himself.
So it was that Jesus said, "My Father worketh hitherto, and I work."
He was continuing to carry out the task of saving mankind.
Jesus did not break the law of the Sabbath;
He was the Lord of the Sabbath, and therefore
He was participating in the work that God the Father was carrying out.

John 5:1-18

[1]After this there was a feast of the Jews; and Jesus went up to Jerusalem. [2]Now there is at Jerusalem by the sheep market a pool, which is called in the Hebrew tongue Bethesda, having five porches. [3]In these lay a great multitude of impotent folk, of blind, halt, withered, waiting for the moving of the water. [4]For an angel went down at a certain season into the pool, and troubled the water: whosoever then first after the troubling of the water stepped in was made whole of whatsoever disease he had.

[5]And a certain man was there, which had an infirmity thirty and eight years. [6]When Jesus saw him lie, and knew that he had been now a long time in that case, he saith unto him, Wilt thou be made whole?

[7]The impotent man answered him, Sir, I have no man, when the water is troubled, to put me into the pool: but while I am coming, another steppeth down before me.

[8]Jesus saith unto him, Rise, take up thy bed, and walk. [9]And immediately the man was made whole, and took up his bed, and walked: and on the same day was the sabbath. [10]The Jews therefore said unto him that was cured, It is the sabbath day: it is not lawful for thee to carry thy bed. [11]He answered them, He that made me whole, the same said unto me, Take up thy bed, and walk.

[12]Then asked they him, What man is that which said unto thee, Take up thy bed, and walk? [13]And he that was healed wist not who it was: for Jesus had conveyed himself away, a multitude being in that place.

[14]Afterward Jesus findeth him in the temple, and said unto him, Behold, thou art made whole: sin no more, lest a worse thing come unto thee. [15]The man departed, and told the Jews that it was Jesus, which had made him whole. [16]And therefore did the Jews persecute Jesus, and sought to slay him, because he had done these things on the sabbath day.

[17]But Jesus answered them, My Father worketh hitherto, and I work. [18]Therefore the Jews sought the more to kill him, because he not only had broken the sabbath, but said also that God was his Father, making himself equal with God.

The Man Who Had an Infirmity for Thirty and Eight Years

This passage is about what happened to a man who had been lying on his sickbed for 38 years. I do not know about you, but I feel a great deal of sympathy for this man, and at the same time, I have great admiration for him. Thirty-eight years! How many people would be able to lie on their backs for such a long time if they were simply told to do so? I have considered from several angles what sort of person this invalid must have been. There are many people in this world who take their own lives rather than face the difficulties they see lying ahead of them. This man, however, suffered for 38 years after he first fell ill. Was it simply a desire to live that led him to persevere for all that time? Or was he so determined to be cured? Or perhaps he was a deep thinker and was waiting in the hope that something might happen.

Another point to be considered here is that Jesus was well aware of this man's situation, and yet He still said to him, "Behold, thou art made whole: sin no more, lest a worse thing come unto thee." If this man had been a punctilious sort of person, no doubt he would have said to Jesus:

"I've been lying here for 38 years; when have I had a chance to run around committing sins?"

This man had been lying there right beside the pool of Bethesda for 38 years unable even to step into the pool, and yet Jesus said to him, "Sin no more." You may wonder if Jesus was perhaps mistaken here in His judgment of this man. It seems to me, however, that Jesus was not just considering this man's physical actions; as He said these words, He was looking deep down inside the man's heart. How many sins can a man commit when he's lying on his back the whole time? Let's take a look at verse 14.

> "Afterward Jesus findeth him in the temple, and said unto him, Behold, thou art made whole: sin no more, lest a worse thing come unto thee."
>
> John 5:14

A person healthy in body and limb would have been able to commit all sorts of sins, since he could move around freely. But this man had simply lain there for 38 years. Since Jesus told such a person to "sin no more," isn't it clear that He was talking not about the sin that is revealed in outward actions but about the heart and the inner activities of the mind? It seems that this is how we should understand these words.

How many Sabbath days[1] would have passed during those 38 years? It must have amounted to quite a number. For this ailing man, the Sabbath was a day on which there was no need even to think about getting into the waters of the pool, since the Jews were strictly forbidden to break the law of the Sabbath. Their law stated clearly that any Jew found working on the Sabbath would be put to death: "Whosoever doeth any work in the Sabbath day, he shall surely be put to death" Exodus 31:15. The fourth commandment was a hard and fast law: "Remember the Sabbath day, to keep it holy" Exodus 20:8.

Over the past 38 years, this man had observed the law regarding the Sabbath day perhaps better than anyone, but then, of all days, Jesus happened to come to the pool of Bethesda on a Sabbath day, and there He led this man to break the law of the Sabbath. It was on a Sabbath day that Jesus healed the man and ordered him to take up his bed and walk. Why did Jesus happen to do such a thing on the Sabbath day?

The Jews were not permitted to walk more than about one kilometer on the Sabbath Day. There was only a certain fixed distance that they were permitted to walk on this day, and they certainly were not allowed to carry their beds as they walked or even to carry so much as a bundle of sticks. Such was the importance of the Sabbath day to the Jews.

This man who had been ill for 38 years had not even been able to lift his own body on the Sabbath day, so he had rested from start to finish. You might say that, at least for those 38 years, this man kept the Sabbath more strictly than any other Jew, since he was lying down the whole time. But then, Jesus suddenly came along and said to this man, "Rise, take up thy bed, and walk." Wasn't Jesus making this man break the law of the Sabbath? He was completely breaking the tradition of the Jews.

Of course when this man took up his pallet and walked, he was obeying Jesus' order and therefore he was not entirely responsible for his actions. Nevertheless, it is a fact that he broke the law of the Sabbath.

A Pool Which Is Called Bethesda

> "After this there was a feast of the Jews; and Jesus went up to Jerusalem."
> John 5:1

The feasts of the Jews were so great that our holidays such as Thanksgiving, New Year, and the Christian feasts of Christmas and Easter do not come anywhere near them by comparison. These were solemn and holy occasions, and the Jews were obliged to keep them. Those Jews who were scattered abroad throughout the world would return to their country at the time of these feasts and go up to Jerusalem to worship there.

> "Now there is at Jerusalem by the sheep market a pool, which is called in the Hebrew tongue Bethesda, having five porches." John 5:2

"Now there is at Jerusalem by the sheep market a pool." The word "market" is used here but other translations use the word "gate."[2] There was an entrance through which the sheep would be brought into the city of Jerusalem, and it seems that near this entrance there was also a sheep market. Every year, many sheep would be brought into Jerusalem through the Sheep Gate to die as offerings in the temple. It was a gate of sacrifice. In other words, this was the gate that was associated with the sheep that were to be offered as sacrifices. Beside this gate there was a pool which in Hebrew was called Bethesda, which means, "house of grace." This pool happened to be beside the Sheep Gate, which seems to have been a very appropriate location.

The pool had five porches. How can I best describe these porches? In recent years, archaeologists have carried out excavations in the area around the city of Jerusalem, and I have seen a photograph of the five porches that were also unearthed in the process of this work. They had large pillars supporting the roof, but there were no walls. At the time of Jesus, there were many sick people lying in these five porches. I read in some book that the number 5, like the other numbers that appear in the Bible, holds a special significance. The book said that it is used to express some kind of grace.

> "In these lay a great multitude of impotent folk, of blind, halt, withered, waiting for the moving of the water. For an angel went down at a certain season into the pool, and troubled the water: whosoever then first after the troubling of the water stepped in was made whole of whatsoever disease he had." John 5:3-4

A crowd of sick people—blind, lame, withered—lay in the porches waiting for the water in the pool to move. It seems that once in a while the waters bubbled up. This happens sometimes, doesn't it? Perhaps you have seen pools of water that suddenly spring up into a fountain in areas around an active volcano. This was probably something similar to that.

> "For an angel went down at a certain season into the pool, and troubled the water: whosoever then first after the troubling of the water stepped in was made whole of whatsoever disease he had." John 5:4

An angel would come and stir up the water. How would it be if a place like this existed today? Whoever entered the waters first was cured of his illness, so how many people do you think would have gathered there? Imagine the scene when the water was stirred up. We read in the Bible about people who suffered from various kinds of illnesses, but these days they would also be joined by people who had been injured in road accidents, forming a huge crowd.

Wilt Thou Be Made Whole?

Whenever this man who had been sick for 38 years tried to make his way to the pool, someone else would jump in ahead of him. How would this man have felt? It was bad enough that he was so ill, but he could not get into the pool first to be healed either. He probably spent a good deal of time lamenting his lot.

We can imagine the scene, can't we? This man waited by the pool, but his chance never came. It was not that the people there waited in line until their turn came. Someone who arrived at the pool a month after this man could have stepped into the waters before him. Then perhaps there was someone who had only just arrived when the waters began to stir, so he jumped in right away. There might even have been someone right next to him who said, "Why don't you go first next time the waters are stirred up," but, when the time came, went ahead of him after all. Under these circumstances, over the years, you would expect this man to have given up all hope.

What would this man's face have looked like after he had been sick for 38 years? Not only would his body have been all twisted, his face would also have been quite contorted. When a person stands up and moves around, his face does not change much even if the skin does begin to sag a bit. When a person lies still for a long period of time, however, his face is pulled back the whole time, and he begins to look completely different. If you take a careful look at the faces of the people around you, you will notice a difference in them between when they are lying down and when they are standing up.

This was a truly pitiful figure of a man, but somehow Jesus' eyes lit on him and He healed him right there and then. You would think that a person with such powers would have been able to heal all the other sick people by the pool as well, but here in John chapter 5 we have the story of just one man. Only the man who had lain ill for 38 years was healed.

> "And a certain man was there, which had an infirmity thirty and eight years. When Jesus saw him lie, and knew that he had been now a long time in that case, he saith unto him, Wilt thou be made whole?"
>
> John 5:5-6

When Jesus asked this question, it was not that He did not know what was in the man's heart, was it? Even before Jesus spoke to him, this man had already lain there for a long time wanting to be healed. It was not because Jesus did not know this that He asked this question.

> "The impotent man answered him, Sir, I have no man, when the water is troubled, to put me into the pool: but while I am coming, another steppeth down before me." .
>
> John 5:7

Now it became clear what kind of help this man needed.

"Sir, I have no one to put me in the pool when the waters are stirred up. Someone needs to carry me and put me in the water, but I don't have anyone like that. So while I'm still on my way someone else steps in before me."

He only said a few words, but they contained all the grievances of this man's life.

Rise, Take up Thy Bed, and Walk

"Jesus saith unto him, Rise, take up thy bed, and walk."   John 5:8

This must have been the first time this man had ever heard such a thing as he lay there on his sickbed. He might often have heard people saying things like:

"How long have you been lying here sick? You poor man!"

"Why don't you read a book or something while you are lying there?"

Or perhaps some more philosophical thinkers might have come along and suggested:

"While you're lying there, look up at the stars, think on them and dream. Broaden your mind a little."

Perhaps there were also some people who came occasionally and gave him a massage. People would have said all kinds of things to this man. In the book of Job, we read that when the man by the name of Job was lying sick, his friends came and said all sorts of things to him, but Job replied:

"Miserable comforters are ye all."   Job 16:2

The words that this man had heard during his 38 years of infirmity probably did not offer him much comfort either. But then, one day, he heard words such as he could never have heard before. No ordinary man could have uttered the words that Jesus now spoke to this man. He said to this man who had lain sick for 38 years, "Rise, take up thy bed, and walk."

"Is this man crazy? I've been lying here sick for 38 years. He must be doing this to provoke me."

Such might have been anyone's reaction.

For this invalid, however, Jesus' words were just right. The words:

"Wilt thou be made whole?"

and:

"Rise, take up thy bed, and walk,"

were the voice of the Son of God who created the heaven and the earth. They were the words of the Creator. This man who had been sick for so long did not waste a moment protesting or complaining that what he was being asked to do was impossible. As soon as he heard these words, he rose to his feet.

This sick man heard words the likes of which he had never heard in his life before, and he was asked a question no one had ever asked him before.

"Wilt thou be made whole?"

This had been the man's life-long wish. It was too tremendous a question to answer. It was too weighty a question for this man to respond to lightly with a simple, "Yes."

> "Sir, I have no man, when the water is troubled, to put me into the pool: but while I am coming, another steppeth down before me."

These words indicate that this was a man who had completely given up. He had no more strength of his own and no more hope. There was only one way out for such a person.

> "Jesus saith unto him, Rise, take up thy bed, and walk." John 5:8

The "bed" that this man took up as he rose had in certain respects been a comfort to him in his illness, but it had also been a place of great torment for him. It had been a burden that he was reluctant to throw away but did not really want to keep. Even so he simply picked it up and walked. Jesus did not tell him to enter the water. He did not have to go to the trouble of doing that.

The Same Day Was the Sabbath

> "And immediately the man was made whole, and took up his bed, and walked: and on the same day was the Sabbath." John 5:9

What day was this? It was the Sabbath day. What do you imagine the Sabbath day to be? Let's turn here to Exodus chapter 20. Let's put all the other laws to one side for a moment and just consider this one law concerning the Sabbath day.

> "Remember the sabbath day, to keep it holy. Six days shalt thou labour, and do all thy work: But the seventh day is the sabbath of the Lord thy God: in it thou shalt not do any work, thou, nor thy son, nor thy daughter, thy manservant, nor thy maidservant, nor thy cattle, nor thy stranger that is within thy gates: For in six days the Lord made heaven and earth, the sea, and all that in them is, and rested the seventh day: wherefore the Lord blessed the sabbath day, and hallowed it." Exodus 20:8-11

No one living under the roof of one of the Israelites was permitted to do any work. Even a cow was not allowed to pull a cart. Absolutely no work was to be done. This is the fourth of the Ten Commandments.

> "Speak thou also unto the children of Israel, saying, Verily my sabbaths ye shall keep: for it is a sign between me and you throughout your generations; that ye may know that I am the Lord that doth sanctify you. Ye shall keep the sabbath therefore; for it is holy unto you: every one that defileth it shall surely be put to death: for whosoever doeth any work therein, that soul shall be cut off from among his people. Six days may work be done; but in the seventh is the sabbath of rest, holy to the Lord: whosoever doeth any work in the sabbath day, he shall surely be put to death. Wherefore the

children of Israel shall keep the sabbath, to observe the sabbath throughout their generations, for a perpetual covenant. It is a sign between me and the children of Israel for ever: for in six days the Lord made heaven and earth, and on the seventh day he rested, and was refreshed."   Exodus 31:13-17

In view of the consequences, do you think it was a trivial matter to break the law of the Sabbath? No, it was an extremely serious matter. The law said very clearly that the Sabbath was not to be broken, and yet it happened to be the Sabbath day when Jesus healed this man. In the eyes of all those present, this was a terrible thing to do. Why did Jesus heal the man on that particular day? This man had passed every Sabbath quietly for the past 38 years without even moving an inch and now, on the Sabbath day, Jesus said to him, "Take up thy bed, and walk."

"The Jews therefore said unto him that was cured, It is the sabbath day: it is not lawful for thee to carry thy bed."   John 5:10

The words of the Jews here were the exact opposite of what Jesus had said to the man. What did Jesus tell him to do? He told him to take up his bed and walk. But what did the Jews say to him?

"It is the Sabbath day; it is not lawful for thee to carry thy bed."

They said it was wrong to do this. The voice of the Son of God and the words of the Son of God were very different from what the Jews said, weren't they? They were the completely opposite.

How would this man have felt when he heard these words? His heart must have skipped a beat, and he probably felt like a man who had received the death sentence. As soon as they said, "It is the Sabbath day," he must have felt that he had already been struck on the back of the head. He had always known that it was not allowed for anyone to do any work at all on the Sabbath day. By leaping up as he had done, he had violated the Sabbath, so the words of the

Jews here must have sounded like thunder to his ears. He probably thought that he was now in big trouble so he immediately came up with an excuse.

Sin No More

> "He answered them, He that made me whole, the same said unto me, Take up thy bed, and walk."
>
> John 5:11

It was not that he himself had decided to walk. He said that someone had told him, "Take up thy bed, and walk," and thus he shifted the blame onto that other Person.

> "Then asked they him, What man is that which said unto thee, Take up thy bed, and walk? And he that was healed wist not who it was: for Jesus had conveyed himself away, a multitude being in that place."
>
> John 5:12-13

The Jews asked the man who it had been that had told him to take up his bed and walk, but the man did not know who had cured him. There was a crowd in that place, so Jesus had already slipped away. That is the way it is when there are a lot of people; a crowd has no sense of responsibility. They probably gathered around the man and applauded, saying, "Wow! A sick man has been cured!" or, "That Man is incredible. Who could He be?" It seems that Jesus found this crowd of people bothersome so He had already slipped away.

> "Afterward Jesus findeth him in the temple, and said unto him, Behold, thou art made whole: sin no more, lest a worse thing come unto thee."
>
> John 5:14

Later, Jesus met this man in the temple. When important events happened in people's lives or their lifelong hopes were accomplished, it was to the temple that they went. This man probably wanted to worship or give an offering in the temple. This seems to be man's nature. There in the temple, Jesus said to the man, "Sin no more, lest a worse thing come unto thee." Since this man had been lying unable to move for 38 years, it may seem that he could not have had anything to do with committing sins. On that day, however, Jesus was indicating that it is man's inner nature to be able to sin even while lying down.

Ever since we were children, we have often been told that we must be good. We learn this in school, we learn it from our parents, and some of you probably also learned it while attending church each Sunday. This is what is taught in many other religions as well. But this is what Jesus said to the Jews who lived their lives strictly according to the law:

> "Ye have heard that it was said by them of old time, Thou shalt not kill; and whosoever shall kill shall be in danger of the judgment: But I say unto you, That whosoever is angry with his brother without a cause shall be in danger of the judgment: and whosoever shall say to his brother, Raca, shall be in danger of the council: but whosoever shall say, Thou fool, shall be in danger of hell fire ... Ye have heard that it was said by them of old time, Thou shalt not commit adultery: But I say unto you, That whosoever looketh on a woman to lust after her hath committed adultery with her already in his heart."
>
> Matthew 5:21-22, 27-28

Jesus was pointing out here that the nature of sin lies in the heart of the individual rather than in his actions. So it is that man is able to sin even while lying perfectly still. This is man's inner nature. Jesus was pointing out the potential for sin that lies within man's nature, the possibility for man to sin within his heart. You may not actually cause harm to another person, but as hatred, jealousy, and envy build up in your heart, the root is always there to give rise to sinful actions. The sins that we commit are simply a result of this sinful nature; every one of us is harboring the source of sin in our hearts.

There is a lesson we can learn from this invalid of 38 years whom Jesus warned about the sinful nature within the heart of man. We may live in our society acting as we please, we may be physically healthy, and we may strive to be moral, religious, and law-abiding, but inwardly, we are no different from this man who had been ill for so long.

They Persecuted Jesus

> "The man departed, and told the Jews that it was Jesus, which had made him whole." John 5:15

After this man had met Jesus in the temple, he went to the Jews to give them an answer. He told them that now he knew who had cured him on that day. Now he knew for sure that it was Jesus.

> "And therefore did the Jews persecute Jesus, and sought to slay him, because he had done these things on the sabbath day." John 5:16

The Jews might have said, "That Man, Jesus, is wicked! Look at what He did to that man who had lain ill for 38 years in the porticoes beside the pool of Bethesda. We have seen how that man has lain still and not moved once on the Sabbath day for the past ten, twenty, or thirty years, but now he has picked up his bed and walked on the Sabbath day. And he says it was Jesus who told him to do this. That Jesus is wicked!" This is probably what the Jews were thinking.

This is how they began to persecute Jesus. Jesus had also provided them with a reason to persecute Him. Let's turn briefly to Numbers in the Old Testament chapter 15.

> "And while the children of Israel were in the wilderness, they found a man that gathered sticks upon the sabbath day. And they that found

him gathering sticks brought him unto Moses and Aaron, and unto all the congregation. And they put him in ward, because it was not declared what should be done to him. And the Lord said unto Moses, The man shall be surely put to death: all the congregation shall stone him with stones without the camp. And all the congregation brought him without the camp, and stoned him with stones, and he died; as the Lord commanded Moses." Numbers 15:32-36

This is a fearful incident, isn't it? The man was dealt with according to the law. When a disagreement arises between two parties, very often it is decided to let the law deal with the matter.

Amongst the laws of the Jews, the commandment to keep the Sabbath day holy demanded very strict observance. When the children of Israel were in the wilderness, there was a man who went to gather wood on the Sabbath day. He became the first sacrifice to this commandment. What did this person do out in the wilderness? He gathered wood and he was put to death for it. He had committed a serious offense. I do not know if people are still stoned for breaking the law of the Sabbath, but orthodox Jews keep these laws very strictly, even to this day.

I once had an opportunity to talk with a young Jew, and it just happened to be on a Friday afternoon. As we were talking, he looked at his watch and then he excused himself. He explained that the Sabbath would begin very soon and hurried off. I was surprised that the Sabbath was still so very important to the Jews.

> "Keep the sabbath day to sanctify it, as the Lord thy God hath commanded thee. Six days thou shalt labour, and do all thy work: But the seventh day is the sabbath of the Lord thy God: in it thou shalt not do any work, thou, nor thy son, nor thy daughter, nor thy manservant, nor thy maidservant, nor thine ox, nor thine ass, nor any of thy cattle, nor thy stranger that is within thy gates; that thy manservant and thy maidservant may rest as well as thou. And

remember that thou wast a servant in the land of Egypt, and that the Lord thy God brought thee out thence through a mighty hand and by a stretched out arm: therefore the Lord thy God commanded thee to keep the sabbath day."
Deuteronomy 5:12-15

Not even a person staying as a visitor was allowed to do any work. This is how strict the law of the Jews was. And they were supposed to keep this law. But Jesus broke it and, in doing this, He was setting Himself up for His death.

He That Is Hanged Is Accursed of God

"And if a man have committed a sin worthy of death, and he be to be put to death, and thou hang him on a tree: His body shall not remain all night upon the tree, but thou shalt in any wise bury him that day; (for he that is hanged is accursed of God;) that thy land be not defiled, which the Lord thy God giveth thee for an inheritance."
Deuteronomy 21:22-23

Anyone who was hanged on a tree was accursed of God. In this passage it says that if a person committed a sin worthy of death, he was to be hanged on a tree until he died, but his body was not to be left there overnight; he was to be buried that same day.

> Were you there when they crucified my Lord?
> Were you there when they crucified my Lord?
>
> Were you there when they laid Him in the tomb?
> Were you there when they laid Him in the tomb?
>
> Oh! Sometimes it causes me to tremble, tremble, tremble,
> Were you there when they crucified my Lord?[3]

Right there! When Jesus was crucified and buried, His body was not left on the cross overnight. On the day of His crucifixion, the soldiers came to Him and found that He was already dead. At that time, the two thieves crucified beside Jesus were still alive, so the soldiers broke the legs of these two men. Since Jesus had already died, however, they did not break His legs. In the Old Testament it says, regarding the slaughter of the Passover lamb, "Neither shall ye break a bone thereof" Exodus 12:46.

The One who hung on the tree was Jesus. The Sabbath day healing of the man who had been ill for 38 years was directly linked with Jesus' death. This man who was healed was also entrusted to Jesus' death. Later, as the apostle Paul spoke of the kind of faith that provides a model for Christians, he said:

> "I am crucified with Christ." Galatians 2:20

Jesus said that He Himself was the Lord of the Sabbath.[4] He also said, "The Sabbath was made for man" Mark 2:27. After Jesus was crucified, He lay in the tomb on the Sabbath day. Jesus covered Himself with the sins of all mankind. Since He took upon Himself the sins of everyone in this world, didn't that make Him a sinner? He became a sinner who took upon Himself the heaviest burden of sin in the world.

> "For as many as are of the works of the law are under the curse: for it is written, Cursed is every one that continueth not in all things which are written in the book of the law to do them. But that no man is justified by the law in the sight of God, it is evident: for, The just shall live by faith. And the law is not of faith: but, The man that doeth them shall live in them. Christ hath redeemed us from the curse of the law, being made a curse for us: for it is written, Cursed is every one that hangeth on a tree." Galatians 3:10-13

For whose sake was Christ cursed? For our sake, He took upon Himself the burden of our sins. It was because Jesus was responsible for the Sabbath that He healed the invalid of 38 years on the Sabbath day. As He told the man, "Take up thy bed, and walk," Jesus was taking upon Himself the responsibility for the Sabbath. So on the day of His crucifixion, Jesus took upon Himself this sick man's burden and all his suffering.

It was not only for the sake of this man; it was for all of us, all of you, and me too. We are all the same as this man who had been sick for 38 years. There is no difference. God worked for six days and on the seventh day He ceased from His labors. He rested. We, however, were living in the midst of sin, without any connection with God whatsoever, and without any rest.

I Am Crucified With Christ

Man was happy in the Garden of Eden. As soon as man sinned, however, he began to live in uneasiness and anxiety. He had lost his paradise, and in this state, descendants were born to him. Just as thorns and thistles awaited Adam in the plains when he was driven out of paradise, we too continually live in the midst of worries, cares, suffering, anguish, and anxiety. God's rest had no opportunity to be able to enter our hearts since we are the descendants of man, the one who broke God's Sabbath.

As man, having broken God's Sabbath rest, wandered in the midst of sin, Jesus took all of man's sins upon Himself and was crucified. While Jesus was living in this world in the flesh, He healed many people of their afflictions; He brought the lame to their feet, and He opened the eyes of the blind. All of these miracles signify that, while we may seem to know God, our eyes are closed and we cannot walk before Him and our spirits are crippled in front of Him. In the Bible we can see how Jesus took all our sins upon Himself as He was crucified and died.

It is for this reason that Jesus said, "My Father worketh hitherto, and I work" John 5:17. The Bible tells us how Jesus carried out the work of fulfilling the prophecies of the Old Testament one by one and then at the end, "He said, It is finished: and he bowed his head, and gave up the ghost" John 19:30.

Let's read the words of the apostle Paul and examine ourselves individually in the light of these words.

> "I am crucified with Christ: nevertheless I live; yet not I, but Christ liveth in me: and the life which I now live in the flesh I live by the faith of the Son of God, who loved me, and gave himself for me."
>
> Galatians 2:20

Try replacing the words, "I" and "me," with your own name as you read this verse. Do these words apply only to those who have a strong faith? No, they do not. We are all included here. When Jesus was crucified, "I" was crucified with Him. This was what led one believer to write the words to the following hymn:

> What can wash away my sin?
> Nothing but the blood of Jesus.
> What can make me whole again?
> Nothing but the blood of Jesus.[5]

Nothing but the blood of Jesus. Each time this same Jesus healed an ailing person, making that person whole on the Sabbath, the Jews wanted to stone Him to death. Instances such as these kept building up until the Jews decided to put Jesus to death, and in the end He was nailed to the cross and died. Jesus was already prepared to meet this death and He continued to carry out His work. Unaware of this, the Jews thought that the only path to righteousness was through strict adherence to the law. Their understanding, however, conflicted with the words of God.

The seventh day was the day of rest. When God created the heaven and the earth, He rested on the seventh day, so He commanded that we too should rest. But how can we rest in such a state? Can we really take a proper rest if our hearts are full of uneasiness and anxiety? When Jesus said that He was the Lord of the Sabbath, He meant that through the cross, He filled the deep chasm between man and God. Jesus said, "I am the way, the truth, and the life" John 14:6. When man sinned, he broke the Sabbath and therefore Jesus took this problem upon Himself. So it was that Jesus said, "My Father worketh hitherto, and I work." He was continuing to carry out the task of saving mankind.

> "And therefore did the Jews persecute Jesus, and sought to slay him, because he had done these things on the sabbath day." John 5:16

Jesus Himself furnished the Jews with a reason to persecute Him. Why do you think He did this? It was because we have all strayed from God's Sabbath, we were unable to keep the Sabbath, and we were under a curse. We were destined for judgment, so Jesus had to undergo the judgment on our behalf.

My Father Worketh Hitherto

> "But Jesus answered them, My Father worketh hitherto, and I work." John 5:17

"My Father worketh hitherto, and I work." He had been working ever since the creation. Let's turn now to Genesis chapter 2.

> "Thus the heavens and the earth were finished, and all the host of them. And on the seventh day God ended his work which he had made; and he rested on the seventh day from all his work which he had made. And God blessed the seventh day, and sanctified it: because that in it he had rested from all his work which God created and made." Genesis 2:1-3

After God created the heavens and the earth, He rested on the seventh day, but His rest was only brief. This was because man sinned. Man ate the fruit of the tree of the knowledge of good and evil, the fruit that God had forbidden him to eat. When God called out, "Adam," the man was already hiding. From the day that man sinned and throughout human history, God has had to continue to carry out the work of saving mankind. This work has prevented God from being able to rest.

What was the first thing that God did? He asked Adam why he had eaten the forbidden fruit. God was teaching Adam something, but Adam made an excuse:

> "The woman whom thou gavest to be with me, she gave me of the tree, and I did eat." Genesis 3:12

Aren't we the same? If you take a look at the members of your own family, you will find that they are very good at making excuses even though no one has taught them to do this. We are all very good at laying the blame on something or someone else. It is not that we learn to do this in school, either. This is something we have inherited from the time of Adam. After eating the fruit of the tree of the knowledge of good and evil, man changed.

God also asked Eve:

"What is this that thou hast done?"

"The serpent beguiled me, and I did eat."

Then God spoke to the serpent:

"I will put enmity between thee and the woman, and between thy seed and her seed; it shall bruise thy head."[6]

With these words, God was explaining the way in which, in the future, mankind would be able to be saved. The work of salvation had begun.

That is not all. God also undertook the task of removing the covering of fig leaves that man, the sinner, had made for himself.

The Bible says that God made coats of skins for the man and his wife and clothed them.[7]

In many places in the Bible we come across references to people using clothing to cover their shame or the parts of the body best not revealed. In the book of Revelation, for example, it says, "I counsel thee to buy of me ... white raiment, that thou mayest be clothed, and that the shame of thy nakedness do not appear" Revelation 3:18, and, "She should be arrayed in fine linen, clean and white: for the fine linen is the righteousness of saints" Revelation 19:8. Also, Isaiah talks about "the robe of righteousness." This is a kind of shadow.

> "I will greatly rejoice in the Lord, my soul shall be joyful in my God; for he hath clothed me with the garments of salvation, he hath covered me with the robe of righteousness, as a bridegroom decketh himself with ornaments, and as a bride adorneth herself with her jewels." Isaiah 61:10

All of God's words and commandments after He drove man out of the Garden of Eden have been intended to bring about man's salvation. All that God said at the time of Noah's flood, at the time of the Tower of Babel, and at the time of Abraham were a part of the process of saving mankind. In order to prepare the way for man to be able to be saved through the Bible, God started off the history of one particular nation through which the Scriptures might be recorded. The Bible tells us that Abraham had a son, and that son also had a son and so on. The list of descendants continues to an almost tedious extent. If it had not been for this succession of births, however, the way could not have been opened for mankind to be saved.

In Matthew chapter 1, it says, "The book of the generation of Jesus Christ, the son of David, the son of Abraham." This genealogy, appearing as it does at the beginning of the New Testament, shows that there was one lineage from Abraham through to Jesus Christ. It was through this lineage that Jesus came and said, "My Father worketh hitherto, and I work."

When He Had Purged Our Sins

In reference to this work of salvation, the apostle Paul wrote:

"God, who at sundry times and in divers manners spake in time past unto the fathers by the prophets, Hath in these last days spoken unto us by his Son, whom he hath appointed heir of all things, by whom also he made the worlds." Hebrews 1:1-2

The Son came and spoke in person. Who is this Son who has appeared "in these last days"? He is the true Light that came into the world. He is the Creator. Even before Jesus Christ, the Son of God, came to this earth, He already existed as the Creator. He was also the Word that was from the beginning. In this Word there was life and there was light, and everything was being accomplished according to this Word. The Word had been proclaimed in advance, telling when Jesus would be born, where He would be born, and to whom He would be born, and then one day the Word radiated light. At the time of Jesus' birth, a star shone in the east, and wise men from the east followed it. Jesus was born in Judea, just as it had been recorded about 1400 years previously: "There shall come a Star out of Jacob, and a Sceptre shall rise out of Israel" Numbers 24:17. The Word appeared precisely as it had been foretold, and Christ was born in accordance with God's word.

"Who being the brightness of his glory, and the express image of his person, and upholding all things by the word of his power, when he had by himself purged our sins, sat down on the right hand of the Majesty on high." Hebrews 1:3

Who is this Person? It is Jesus. Christ came in accordance with the words of the Old Testament, which God had already prepared long before in order to bring about the salvation of mankind. That is why the apostle Peter wrote:

> "Of which salvation the prophets have enquired and searched diligently, who prophesied of the grace that should come unto you: Searching what, or what manner of time the Spirit of Christ which was in them did signify, when it testified beforehand the sufferings of Christ, and the glory that should follow." 1 Peter 1:10-11

King David wrote:

> "My God, my God, why hast thou forsaken me? … the assembly of the wicked have inclosed me: they pierced my hands and my feet. … they look and stare upon me. They part my garments among them, and cast lots upon my vesture." Psalm 22:1, 16-18

These words that David recorded were fulfilled in later days when Jesus hung on the cross. The prophets had already written about Christ's sufferings and the glory that would follow.

After the death of a great person, people of later generations write biographies in admiration of that person. In the case of Jesus, however, His aim in coming to this world, His will, and His plan were all recorded beforehand. This has been true of no one else in the history of mankind. Jesus alone was born in accordance with prophecies made in advance. He was the Savior who came to the world to save mankind. This is why He was able to say, "My Father worketh hitherto, and I work."

> "I am the way, the truth, and the life: no man cometh unto the Father, but by me." John 14:6

In order to open the way to the Father referred to in this verse, Jesus had to stand on the path of death. He died in order to give the Sabbath rest to man's spirit. On the day that man sinned, God said to him, "In the sweat of thy face shalt thou eat bread" Genesis 3:19. From that time on, man has lived in the midst of suffering and afflictions, unable to find the true Sabbath, so Jesus had to die on the cross to bring rest to mankind.

When Jesus said, "My Father worketh hitherto, and I work," He meant that He was carrying out the task of saving mankind. Jesus did not break the law of the Sabbath; He was the Lord of the Sabbath, and therefore He was participating in the work that God the Father was carrying out. The healing of the man who had lain sick for 38 years was a shadow of Jesus' work of saving the spirits of men. This one man was healed as a model of how we come to receive the Sabbath rest in our spirits.

They Sought the More to Kill Jesus

> "Therefore the Jews sought the more to kill him, because he not only had broken the sabbath, but said also that God was his Father, making himself equal with God." John 5:18

"This Man dares to say that God is His Father!" The Jews were outraged and simply could not tolerate Jesus. "How dare He, a mere man, place Himself on equal standing with God?" They could hardly believe their ears. In the eyes of the Jews, people who adhered strictly to the law, Jesus had to be put to death no matter what it took.

For man to keep the Sabbath, it was merely a case of acting according to the law, and this was also true when they violated the

Sabbath, but Jesus had said that His Father had been working until now and He Himself was working. To the Jews, it seemed that Jesus had elevated Himself to the status of the Creator and was telling people what to do.

The Jews could not help but despise Jesus and consider His words and actions inexcusable. They had found a pretext for His death. This was the path to Jesus' death; He had already prepared this path. One by one, Jesus was building up a store of deeds that would lead the Jews to the stage where they could stand it no longer and would have to put Him to death. Such was the curse that was upon Jesus—because of us, sinners.

Many people think of Jesus' suffering as being merely His crucifixion, the agony of the iron nails piercing His hands and feet and the crown of thorns on His head. If we look into the matter more deeply, however, we find that His death was being prepared long before that. Gradually, the hammer and nails and the wood for the cross were being prepared in accordance with the prophecies that had been made at many times and in many ways in the Old Testament.

> "Let this mind be in you, which was also in Christ Jesus: Who, being in the form of God, thought it not robbery to be equal with God: But made himself of no reputation, and took upon him the form of a servant, and was made in the likeness of men: And being found in fashion as a man, he humbled himself, and became obedient unto death, even the death of the cross." Philippians 2:5-8

In what form does it say that Jesus came? Although He was in the form of God, He made Himself of no reputation and was found in the form of a servant. He left behind His godly form and came in the body of a man. He had to come in exactly the same form as man if He was to take upon Himself the sins of man.

Who Gave Himself a Ransom For All

> "Who will have all men to be saved, and to come unto the knowledge of the truth. For there is one God, and one mediator between God and men, the man Christ Jesus; Who gave himself a ransom for all, to be testified in due time." 1 Timothy 2:4-6

Anyone who reads these verses precisely can be assured of being a child of God on this earth. The Bible says that there is just one Mediator between God and men. However, there are many people who believe in God the Father, God the Son, and God the Holy Spirit, and yet establish some other mediator between God and men. This is terrible but it is true. There is no other mediator between God and men. The only Mediator is the Man Jesus Christ who was crucified and rose from the dead.

In the Bible it says, "Neither is there is salvation in any other:no one else; for there is none other name under heaven given among men, whereby we must be saved" Acts 4:12. Nevertheless, there are a tremendous number of people in the world today who do not know what true salvation is or what the real truth is. A grateful spirit within an apparently insignificant person is more precious than the magnificent singing of a world-famous choir in a splendidly adorned church building. Where else will the kingdom of God be, but in the heart of the individual who realizes, "You, Lord, are my Mediator"?

> In cottage or a mansion fair,
> Where Jesus is 'tis Heaven there.[8]

This is precisely what is meant by the truth of the gospel—the gospel of truth.

What happened to the invalid of 38 years after he had taken up his bed and walked? He saw the Jews cursing and verbally attacking the Man who had healed him. He also heard the words of this Man. The same words that have reached across the past two thousand years as far as us also reached the ears of this insignificant invalid.

Similarly, today, sinners such as we are, can hear the words of the gospel that was recorded at that time. So it is that God has declared us to be righteous. If God acknowledges us as being righteous, who can condemn us? We have never received God's holy law; neither have we ever observed it. In the eyes of the law, we are sinners destined without fail for judgment, but we have been saved by grace. Shouldn't we be people who can be thankful before God for this grace? There are many people in this world whose spirits are just drifting along, not knowing where they are going.

"All we like sheep have gone astray; we have turned every one to his own way; and the Lord hath laid on him the iniquity of us all."
Isaiah 53:6

"There is a way that seemeth right unto a man, but the end thereof are the ways of death." Proverbs 16:25

Many people are walking on this path of death.

> What a wonderful change in my life has been wrought
> Since Jesus came into my heart.
> ...
> There's a light in the valley of death now for me
> Since Jesus came into my heart.[9]

The time came when each of us individually experienced a joy we had never known before. "Oh, that is true! Now I believe!" This does not come from ourselves; it is the heart that God has given us.

"Let this mind be in you, which was also in Christ Jesus." Philippians 2:5

God's Sabbath begins within the individual from the moment the peace that God gives enters the heart. It is as the Bible says, "Though thou wast angry with me, thine anger is turned away" Isaiah 12:1. Now God's anger has turned away from us.

211

15

Eternal Life and Eternal Punishment

John 5:19-29

Who has received the authority to judge?
Jesus has.
Since Jesus came in the form of a man, He knew all the things of men.
He understood man's situation, man's sin, and man's sufferings.
Since Jesus has received the judgment in our place,
He is qualified to stand boldly before man.
Some day, everyone will hear His voice,
both those who have performed good deeds
and those who have been engaged in evil.
All the people who have ever lived will be divided into two groups—
those who have come forth to the resurrection of life
and those who have come forth to the resurrection of damnation.

John 5:19-29

[19]Then answered Jesus and said unto them, Verily, verily, I say unto you, The Son can do nothing of himself, but what he seeth the Father do: for what things soever he doeth, these also doeth the Son likewise. [20]For the Father loveth the Son, and sheweth him all things that himself doeth: and he will shew him greater works than these, that ye may marvel. [21]For as the Father raiseth up the dead, and quickeneth them; even so the Son quickeneth whom he will. [22]For the Father judgeth no man, but hath committed all judgment unto the Son: [23]That all men should honour the Son, even as they honour the Father. He that honoureth not the Son honoureth not the Father which hath sent him.

[24]Verily, verily, I say unto you, He that heareth my word, and believeth on him that sent me, hath everlasting life, and shall not come into condemnation; but is passed from death unto life.

[25]Verily, verily, I say unto you, The hour is coming, and now is, when the dead shall hear the voice of the Son of God: and they that hear shall live. [26]For as the Father hath life in himself; so hath he given to the Son to have life in himself; [27]And hath given him authority to execute judgment also, because he is the Son of man. [28]Marvel not at this: for the hour is coming, in the which all that are in the graves shall hear his voice, [29]And shall come forth; they that have done good, unto the resurrection of life; and they that have done evil, unto the resurrection of damnation.

For What Things Soever the Father Doeth, These also Doeth the Son Likewise

> "Then answered Jesus and said unto them, Verily, verily, I say unto you, The Son can do nothing of himself, but what he seeth the Father do: for what things soever he doeth, these also doeth the Son likewise." John 5:19

Why did Jesus emphasize His words here to the point of saying, "Verily, verily"? There was not a single lie contained in the words that Jesus spoke.

> "The Son can do nothing of himself, but what he seeth the Father do."

Here Jesus was not talking about an ordinary family in this world in which the son watches his father's actions and does the same. All the prophecies in the Old Testament brought about Jesus' birth, and all the works that Jesus was to carry out were explained one by one in the Old Testament. These living words gave birth to Jesus Christ who brought the New Testament to completion. Since Jesus had come in accordance with God's word, He said that He did not act on His own initiative, but did what He saw His Father doing. When He said, "The Son can do nothing of himself, but what he seeth the Father do," He meant that He was acting in accordance with the words recorded in the Old Testament.

Jesus often used the expression, "It is written." When the devil was tempting Him, He said, "It is written, Man shall not live by bread alone, but by every word that proceedeth out of the mouth of God" Matthew 4:4. He answered the devil with words from the Old Testament.[1]

> "For the Father loveth the Son, and sheweth him all things that himself doeth: and he will shew him greater works than these, that ye may marvel." John 5:20

Here Jesus was saying that God would show them even greater works than they had witnessed so far, works at which they would marvel and say, "This is it!"

> "For as the Father raiseth up the dead, and quickeneth them; even so the Son quickeneth whom he will." John 5:21

In the Old Testament, there were times when God used a prophet to bring someone back to life. From time to time, while Jesus was on this earth, He also brought a dead person back to life. In such cases, God set to work at the point where human powers could do no more. Thus God gave life to those who were completely given up for dead. When Jesus raised a girl whom others had declared dead, He said, "The maid is not dead, but sleepeth."[2]

Why did Jesus say this? The Bible says, "For all live unto [God]" Luke 20:38.

God is able to raise everyone, even from death. On the day of the final judgment, there will be the resurrection of the good and the resurrection of the wicked. At that time, God will raise up two kinds of people—those who will enter the eternal heavenly kingdom and those who will enter the place of eternal punishment. He has entrusted this work to Jesus, His Son. When Jesus said, "Even so the Son quickeneth whom he will," we can understand this to mean that when people living on this earth listen to the words of God, and the Holy Spirit comes upon them, their spirits come alive. The Son of God came in the body of a man in order to explain this matter of eternal life and death.

The Father Hath Committed All Judgment unto the Son

> "For the Father judgeth no man, but hath committed all judgment unto the Son." John 5:22

Eternal Life and Eternal Punishment

These are really tremendous words. The Father does not judge anyone; He has put His Son in charge of the judgment. Since the Son has already come and received the power of judgment in all things, in the future too, everything will come about as it has been recorded in the Bible. In the Old Testament, God said, "There shall no man see me, and live" Exodus 33:20. If God Himself were to judge man, it would be truly terrifying, wouldn't it? His Son, on the other hand, was very close to man. He came into physical contact and conversed with man. It was to this Son that God entrusted all judgment.

Some people say that they do not believe in Jesus, but they believe in God. People like this ought to consider the Bible verse that says, "Thou believest that there is one God; thou doest well: the devils also believe, and tremble" James 2:19. Those who believe in God but exclude Jesus have the kind of faith that will take them to hell. Some day, when God reveals Jesus to them, they will be shocked and terrified.

Therefore, we must all come closer to Jesus before that day comes. How do all the people of this world perceive Jesus? Before we start thinking of Him simply as being the Man depicted hanging on the cross on top of a church spire, we need to know precisely who He is. From John chapter 5 verse 19 on, Jesus discloses exactly who He is. It is impossible to find out who Jesus is by using the methods of inquiry adopted in our world in order to establish the identity of an individual. In the eyes of man, Jesus was a Man, but who dwelt within Him?

"He that hath seen me hath seen the Father." John 14:9

Jesus said that there is no difference between seeing Him and seeing God. Can we see the love of a mother with our physical eyes? There is an old Korean song that says:

217

> As high as the sky above may be,
> There is something even higher,
> The love of the one who bore and raised me,
> My mother.

We may sing of all that a mother does for her child, but we cannot see the actual love itself. Can we see love through a microscope? Can we use a measuring instrument to gauge love? And yet love does exist. Even though we cannot see it, it is there. How can we see the love of God? If we are not careful, we may make the mistake of looking only at Jesus' death and thus become discouraged. But God raised Jesus from the dead.

> "[Jesus] was delivered for our offences, and was raised again for our justification." Romans 4:25

Who raised Jesus? It was God who raised Him.

> I know not why God's wondrous grace to me He hath made known,
> Nor why, unworthy, Christ in love Redeemed me for His own.
>
> I know not how this saving faith to me He did impart,
> Nor how believing in His Word, wrought peace within my heart.
>
> I know not how the Spirit moves, convincing men of sin,
> Revealing Jesus through the Word, creating faith in Him.
>
> I know not what of good or ill may be reserved for me,
> Of weary ways of golden days, before His face I see.
>
> Refrain:
> But "I know whom I have believed, and am persuaded that He is able
> To keep that which I've committed unto Him against that day."[3]

Jesus taught us that He Himself was God. He was God Himself who made Himself visible to man. He was God who came into the world in the form of a man.

According to John chapter 5 verse 22, who has received the authority to judge? It is Jesus, isn't it? Since Jesus came in the form of a man, He knew all the things of men. He understood man's situation, man's sin, and man's sufferings. Therefore He is fully qualified to stand before man as judge. He has this authority. God did not appear to man in person; He revealed Himself to the prophets through the Holy Spirit, and the prophets passed God's words on to other people. Now, however, Jesus has appeared to mankind in person in accordance with the Old Testament scriptures proclaimed by the prophets.

My Wellbeloved Hath a Vineyard

> "That all men should honour the Son, even as they honour the Father. He that honoureth not the Son honoureth not the Father which hath sent him."
> John 5:23

Let's suppose the king of a certain country had a son. That son would be the prince, wouldn't he? If the citizens of that country liked their king, would they be able to treat the prince with contempt? They wouldn't, would they? As we read through the Old Testament, we find that God often speaks in parables to make it easy for us to understand. To give you an example, there is a verse that says:

> "Take us the foxes, the little foxes, that spoil the vines: for our vines have tender grapes."
> The Song of Solomon 2:15

The grapes are still young and tender but it seems the little foxes have made a hole in the fence and come into the vineyard, thinking they might find something to eat. The foxes have come in and are running wild, ruining the tender young grapes. If the foxes trample the young grapes, there will not be any good fruit.

So the prophet said, "Take us the foxes, the little foxes, that spoil the vines." There are little foxes that spoil the vines. In other words, there is an obstructive element in the vineyard. What does this vineyard signify?

In the New Testament there is also a parable about a vineyard. It tells of a certain landowner who planted a vineyard on his land and surrounded it with a fence. In the vineyard he built a high tower and a big winepress. Then he rented the vineyard out to some vine-growers. This represents how God chose one nation—the Israelites—from among all the nations on this earth and promised that the Messiah would be born amongst their descendants.

> "And there shall come forth a rod out of the stem of Jesse, and a Branch shall grow out of his roots: And the spirit of the Lord shall rest upon him, the spirit of wisdom and understanding, the spirit of counsel and might, the spirit of knowledge and of the fear of the Lord." Isaiah 11:1-2

Amongst the descendants of Judah, one particular Person, described here as "a rod," would come forth from the stem of Jesse. This rod is Jesus Christ, the Son of God. The One who would come forth from the vine is Jesus. So in John chapter 15 Jesus said, "I am the vine, ye are the branches" John 15:5. Let's take a look at the vineyard that appears in the writings of the prophet Isaiah.

> "Now will I sing to my wellbeloved a song of my beloved touching his vineyard. My wellbeloved hath a vineyard in a very fruitful hill: And he fenced it, and gathered out the stones thereof, and planted it with the choicest vine, and built a tower in the midst of it, and also made a winepress therein: and he looked that it should bring forth grapes, and it brought forth wild grapes." Isaiah 5:1-2

These verses describe the fate of the Israelites. Here, "my wellbeloved" is God, and the vineyard is the Israelites.

> "And now, O inhabitants of Jerusalem, and men of Judah, judge, I pray you, betwixt me and my vineyard. What could have been done more to my vineyard, that I have not done in it? wherefore, when I looked that it should bring forth grapes, brought it forth wild grapes? And now go to; I will tell you what I will do to my vineyard: I will take away the hedge thereof, and it shall be eaten up; and break down the wall thereof, and it shall be trodden down: And I will lay it waste: it shall not be pruned, nor digged; but there shall come up briers and thorns: I will also command the clouds that they rain no rain upon it. For the vineyard of the Lord of hosts is the house of Israel, and the men of Judah his pleasant plant: and he looked for judgment, but behold oppression; for righteousness, but behold a cry."
> Isaiah 5:3-7

> "For the vineyard of the Lord of hosts is the house of Israel, and the men of Judah his pleasant plant."

God wanted the Israelites to produce good grapes, but they produced wild grapes. So God stopped the rain from falling on the vineyard, took away the hedge, and broke down the wall. Events in the history of Israel turned out exactly as these verses predicted.

When Jesus came to the land of Israel, the Jews were waiting for the Messiah, but their hearts were in all the wrong places. This was why Jesus said:

> "I thank thee, O Father, Lord of heaven and earth, because thou hast hid these things from the wise and prudent, and hast revealed them unto babes."
> Matthew 11:25

On another occasion, He also said to the Jews:

> "If ye were blind, ye should have no sin: but now ye say, We see; therefore your sin remaineth."
> John 9:41

He that Honoureth Not the Son

Let's turn to Matthew chapter 21. This is where we find the parable of the vineyard that I talked about earlier. This parable also appears in the Gospels of Mark and Luke. The story differs slightly depending on the writer, but the overall message is the same. When the Jews heard Jesus tell this parable, they must have been startled.

> "Hear another parable: There was a certain householder, which planted a vineyard, and hedged it round about, and digged a winepress in it, and built a tower, and let it out to husbandmen, and went into a far country." Matthew 21:33

There was a parable about a vineyard in the Old Testament as well, wasn't there? Now Jesus came in person and spoke again about a vineyard. A certain landowner planted a vineyard, rented it out to tenant farmers, and went off to a distant land. It must have been very hard work to plant the vineyard. The landowner would have had to dig the ground, fertilize it, plant the vines, and build a strong fence around it. When he had finished, he rented out the vineyard to some farmers. These farmers would have been able to keep some of the fruits of their labors, but they would also have had to give a portion of the produce to the landowner.

> "And when the time of the fruit drew near, he sent his servants to the husbandmen, that they might receive the fruits of it. And the husbandmen took his servants, and beat one, and killed another, and stoned another. Again, he sent other servants more than the first: and they did unto them likewise. But last of all he sent unto them his son, saying, They will reverence my son. But when the husbandmen saw the son, they said among themselves, This is the heir; come, let us kill him, and let us seize on his inheritance. And they caught him, and cast him out of the vineyard, and slew him. When the lord therefore of the vineyard cometh, what will he do unto those husbandmen? They say unto him, He will miserably destroy those wicked men, and

will let out his vineyard unto other husbandmen, which shall render him the fruits in their seasons."
Matthew 21:34-41

When the harvest time approached, the landowner sent his servants to the tenant farmers to receive his share of the produce. When the servants arrived, however, the farmers gave them a thorough beating and sent them away. Later, the landowner sent even more servants to them, but again the farmers beat them and this time they killed them. Finally the landowner sent his son, thinking that the farmers would show him some respect, but they seized him as well; they threw him out of the vineyard and killed him. What would the landowner do in such a situation? Wouldn't he annihilate the farmers and rent the vineyard to other vine-growers who would offer him the produce at the proper time? This is a parable that Jesus told. The story of the vineyard that is told here again in the New Testament explains a page in the history of Israel.

> "Jesus saith unto them, Did ye never read in the scriptures, The stone which the builders rejected, the same is become the head of the corner: this is the Lord's doing, and it is marvellous in our eyes? Therefore say I unto you, The kingdom of God shall be taken from you, and given to a nation bringing forth the fruits thereof. And whosoever shall fall on this stone shall be broken: but on whomsoever it shall fall, it will grind him to powder. And when the chief priests and Pharisees had heard his parables, they perceived that he spake of them. But when they sought to lay hands on him, they feared the multitude, because they took him for a prophet."
> Matthew 21:42-46

Receiving Jesus is knowing that He is the stone which the builders rejected and which has become the head of the corner.

Long by the prophets of Israel foretold!
Hail to the millions from bondage returning!
Gentiles and Jews the blest vision behold.[4]

What is the blest vision that was long foretold by the prophets of Israel? It is knowing Jesus. It is meeting Jesus. This is why Jesus quoted here from Psalm 118 verse 22 when He said, "Did ye never read in the scriptures, The stone which the builders rejected, the same is become the head of the corner?" "Haven't you ever heard this?" Jesus said that those who stumble on this stone would be broken to pieces, and those upon whom this rock falls would be ground to powder and scattered like dust. When the chief priests and the Pharisees heard this, they became angry and wanted to arrest Jesus, but they hesitated because they were afraid of the crowd. Jesus told this parable just before He died—it seems that it was probably about three days before His death. It is extremely significant that it was so close to the time when Jesus would have to face His death that He said these words: "But last of all he sent unto them his son, saying, They will reverence my son. But when the husbandmen saw the son, … they caught him, and cast him out of the vineyard, and slew him." This is because this story reflects the scene in which Jesus, the Christ, would be killed.

Jesus bore the cross and died. It was with His death in mind that Jesus told how the landowner had thought that if he sent his son the farmers would honor him, but they threw him outside the vineyard and killed him. In the same way, the Jews had Jesus put to death on the hill of Golgotha, outside the city walls.

> "That all men should honour the Son, even as they honour the Father. He that honoureth not the Son honoureth not the Father which hath sent him." John 5:23

"He that honoureth not the Son honoureth not the Father which hath sent him." Now we can see all that was in the hearts of these people, can't we? Those who do not honor Jesus do not honor God the Father. Jesus fully revealed His identity and His position. Anyone who wants to honor Jesus must listen to His words, but not everyone has the ears to hear.

> "But blessed are your ... ears, because they hear." Matthew 13:16

Anyone hearing these words for the first time might think, "Why would He say something like that? Who doesn't have ears? Did anyone plug up their ears?" But that is not what Jesus meant here. There are people who cannot hear even though they have ears. Jesus once said, "He who has ears to hear, let him hear." He was talking about those who have ears to hear and understand.

Hath Everlasting life

> "Verily, verily, I say unto you, He that heareth my word, and believeth on him that sent me, hath everlasting life, and shall not come into condemnation; but is passed from death unto life." John 5:24

Why did Jesus use the word, "verily," twice here? Once would have been enough. It seems to me that He said it once for the Old Testament and once for the New Testament. In the Old Testament, God explained the method by which man receives new life, and then in the New Testament, Jesus came and provided this new life.

When Jesus said, "I say unto you," many people understand these words to be addressed to everyone in general. Sometimes people read the Bible in this way and miss out on something as they take words that were intended for them personally and think of them as applying to other people. The words, "Verily, verily, I say unto you," are addressed to each one of us individually. Those who have ears to hear will come to listen, won't they?

> "He that heareth my word."

Jesus was God who came to this earth in the body of a man. Hearing the words of Jesus is hearing the voice of God through Jesus.

> "He that heareth my word, and believeth on him that sent me, hath everlasting life."

Do we receive eternal life after we die, or while we are still alive? These words have become universal and many people have heard them, but there are also many people who do not understand what they actually mean. Not everyone has this eternal life, do they? If you know this truth for certain, it is your responsibility to pass it on to your family, your relatives, and the people around you who do not know it. Let's read verse 24 again.

> "Verily, verily, I say unto you, He that heareth my word, and believeth on him that sent me, hath everlasting life, and shall not come into condemnation; but is passed from death unto life." John 5:24

"I have taken your death upon Myself. And in return you have passed into eternal life." Since Jesus has received the judgment in our place, death has now been removed from us. We have also been made exempt from the eternal judgment that will some day take place. The words, "but is passed from death unto life," bring to mind what it says in Romans chapter 6 verse 23:

> "For the wages of sin is death; but the gift of God is eternal life through Jesus Christ our Lord."

The moment Adam sinned, we all came under death, but now we have been given the gift of eternal life that is in Christ. When it says in this verse that we have "passed from death unto life," it means that the eternal judgment has been exchanged for an eternal blessing. Even though Jesus Himself said these words, there are many people who are unable to realize what He was saying because they do not have the ears to hear.

Think about this. By one means or another, we come to see or hear through the Bible that the Son of God came to this earth and saved us, and we realize, "Ah! This is how I am saved. I have been forgiven!" When we come to the Lord in this way, when we come to know and believe in His love, the Holy Spirit comes to us. The Holy Spirit does not just come at any time

The Hour Is Coming and Now Is

> "Verily, verily, I say unto you, The hour is coming, and now is, when the dead shall hear the voice of the Son of God: and they that hear shall live."
>
> John 5:25

This was the case when Jesus said these words, and it is just the same today. The "hour" referred to in this verse is different from any other hour. This "hour" is the moment when people discover that Jesus was the Messiah who appears in the Old Testament and come to believe in God's love.

At the wedding in Cana, when Mary said that they had no wine, Jesus replied, "Woman, ... mine hour is not yet come," didn't He? But here, He said that the hour "now is." It is right now.

Who is referred to as "the dead" in this verse? It includes everyone, since all are dead in Adam. Didn't God say to Adam, the first man, "But of the tree of the knowledge of good and evil, thou shalt not eat of it: for in the day that thou eatest thereof thou shalt surely die" Genesis 2:17? God said, "Thou shalt surely die," but the devil said, "Ye shall not surely die." Eve was deceived by the devil and said, "Lest ye die." She began to doubt and so she ended up eating the fruit of the tree of the knowledge of good and evil.

"The hour is coming, and now is, when the dead shall hear the voice of the Son of God."

Even though we breathe, speak, and move around in this world, we are actually dead. Let's think about it this way. When we turn on the television, we see people who died years ago and yet they appear on the screen moving around and speaking. Even though they are dead, we see them moving around, but that does not mean that they are alive, does it? People live on this earth, communicating with one another, making business transactions, going to school, forming families, and all these actions make them appear to be alive, but in

God's eyes and from His eternal perspective, they are dead. That is not to say that they have stopped breathing in a physical sense; their fellowship and communication with God has been severed. The apostle Paul addressed those who are dead in this sense with the following words:

> "And you hath he quickened, who were dead in trespasses and sins; Wherein in time past ye walked according to the course of this world, according to the prince of the power of the air, the spirit that now worketh in the children of disobedience." Ephesians 2:1-2

In the past, we all walked and lived in this dead state. Even though we were such sinners, however, God, in His abundant mercy and because of His great love with which He loved us, has granted us eternal life. We were dead in our trespasses and sins, but He has made us alive together with Christ.[5]

> "Verily, verily, I say unto you, He that heareth my word, and believeth on him that sent me, hath everlasting life."

Does it say that the believer "will have" eternal life? No, it does not. It says that the believer already "has" eternal life.

> "And shall not come into condemnation; but is passed from death unto life."

The Bible says, "The days of our years are threescore years and ten; and if by reason of strength they be fourscore years, yet is their strength labour and sorrow" Psalm 90:10. Such are our lives, but in the midst of all this emptiness and futility, God has given us an eternal life. He has given us an eternal promise.

> "The hour is coming, and now is, when the dead shall hear the voice of the Son of God: and they that hear shall live."

> "The hour is coming, and now is."

> "Behold, now is the accepted time; behold, now is the day of salvation."
> 2 Corinthians 6:2

If, at any time, or any hour, a person comes to accept Christ through God's word, he receives eternal life. How, then, do we know that we have received eternal life?

In the past, we could not believe, no matter how much effort we put into it or how much we tried to memorize verses from the Bible, but then one day we have the experience of coming to believe. Then we are able to say, "Now, I get it! Now I believe!" It is not by our own efforts that we come to believe in this way; God brings us to such faith.

And Hath Given Him Authority to Execute Judgment

> "For as the Father hath life in himself; so hath he given to the Son to have life in himself."
> John 5:26

Since God is eternal and has eternal life, and since the Father and the Son are equal, God gave this same eternal life to His Son. The Son also had God's life and He is the One who gives us eternal life.

> "And hath given him authority to execute judgment also, because he is the Son of man."
> John 5:27

Who is the Son of Man? He is the Messiah, Jesus Christ, the Son of the living God. God has given His Son the authority to execute judgment. The Son is the One who died on the cross in the place of all mankind. To those who do not believe this, He will no doubt say, "Why didn't you believe? Look at My hands."

When God existed in His intrinsic form as God, He did not manifest to mankind His authority to execute judgment. It was because Jesus came to man in the body of a man, and received judgment from man, that He was given the authority to judge man. He met people on this earth and spoke with them face to face. So it is determined on this earth whether or not we believe in Him. Whether we receive the blessing of being able to go to heaven or the curse of not being able to go is decided while we are living in this world. If you have come to a firm belief in Jesus while living in this world, it will make no difference where or how you die. The problem of eternal life is solved on this earth.

The Resurrection of Life and the Resurrection of Damnation

> "Marvel not at this: for the hour is coming, in the which all that are in the graves shall hear his voice, And shall come forth; they that have done good, unto the resurrection of life; and they that have done evil, unto the resurrection of damnation." John 5:28-29

A while ago, I heard some Christians singing a hymn. The words of the hymns were so strange that I wondered if the writer had really understood the Bible before he wrote the hymn. It seems it was one of those new contemporary hymns and it included the line, "If I were born into this world again." These are words that cannot exist in Christianity. We cannot be born into this world again. Once we leave this world, that is it. In the course of our lives, we sometimes wish we could go back to the days of our childhood, but that is also just a dream.

A long time ago one Korean poet expressed this point very well:

> Sweet briar of Myongsa-Shimri
> Grieve not for your fading blooms.
> When the spring comes next March, they will bloom again,
> But woe! Once our lives pass, they never return.

Life passes and does not come around again.

"And as it is appointed unto men once to die, but after this the judgment."
Hebrews 9:27

No other theory is acceptable. Also, someday all the dead will rise again. The time will come when all those in their tombs will hear His voice. That will be the Day of Judgment. When a person comes to the end of his life in this world and his spirit leaves his body, the body decays, but God stores the spirit away until the day of the Last Judgment when He will awaken all the dead. At that time, two types of resurrection will take place: the resurrection of those who have done evil and that of those who have done good.

"The hour is coming, in the which all that are in the graves shall hear his voice." Everyone will hear His voice, both those who have performed good deeds and those who have been engaged in evil. There are two types of people who have died and been buried— those who have come to believe in Jesus and those who have not— and some day they will all be resurrected in the flesh. At that time, all the people who have ever lived will be divided into those two groups and either be included amongst those who have come forth to the resurrection of life or those who have come forth to the resurrection of damnation. Those who come forth to the resurrection of life will go to the eternal heavenly kingdom, while those who come forth to the resurrection of damnation will remain under the sentence of death and rise to face eternal torment in hell. There are those who suffer shame and everlasting contempt, and there are those who receive eternal life.

Jesus was explaining that these two types of resurrection would take place. Even while He was on this earth, Jesus was judging between those who had the assurance that they could go to heaven and those who did not have this assurance.

"And many of them that sleep in the dust of the earth shall awake, some to everlasting life, and some to shame and everlasting contempt. And they that be wise shall shine as the brightness of the firmament; and they that turn many to righteousness as the stars for ever and ever." Daniel 12:2-3

This verse refers to "them that sleep in the dust of the earth"; that is, in the soil. In other words, it is talking about those who sleep in the ground. It also says here that some shall awake to everlasting life. Let's consider what it says here about everlasting life and compare it with what it says in John chapter 5 verse 24: "He that heareth my word, and believeth on him that sent me, hath everlasting life." In John chapter 5 verse 24, Jesus gave the promise of eternal life to be received while we are living in this world. Daniel chapter 12 verse 2, on the other hand, is talking about those people who will enter into eternal life at the time of the Last Judgment.

Both those who have received eternal life and those who have not will remain buried in the ground until the day comes for them to rise from their tombs. Those who have received everlasting life will live on forever by the power of the eternal life they have received. Those who have not received eternal life will rise in their condemned state and go to the place of eternal judgment.

We were born into this world in order to receive eternal life, this eternal blessing, this everlasting promise.

When They Hear His Voice

> "For the hour is coming, in the which all that are in the graves shall hear his voice." John 5:28

This verse says that all will hear His voice, but this does not mean that everyone will hear it at the same time. There is a great difference in time between the hour when those who have received eternal life will hear His voice and the hour when those who have not will hear it. There is a hymn that includes the line, "When the trumpet of the Lord shall sound and time shall be no more." We do not know exactly when it will be, but the day will come when the heavens will open and those who are to enjoy the eternal blessing will be taken up to heaven. First those who are asleep in Christ will arise and immediately after that those who remain on the earth will be taken up. The people who have received eternal life will hear the Lord calling and be taken up.

The apostle Paul wrote:

"For this we say unto you by the word of the Lord, that we which are alive and remain unto the coming of the Lord shall not prevent them which are asleep. For the Lord himself shall descend from heaven with a shout, with the voice of the archangel, and with the trump of God: and the dead in Christ shall rise first: Then we which are alive and remain shall be caught up together with them in the clouds, to meet the Lord in the air: and so shall we ever be with the Lord. Wherefore comfort one another with these words."

1 Thessalonians 4:15-18

We learn, know, and believe verses like these, and then someday we will be taken up just as these living words say. Those who have not received God's words of life and do not have these words accomplished within them will not be able to go when Jesus calls. If they have never heard Him say, "Come," how will they be able to go? Those who are not called at that time will remain as they are in their graves until they are summoned at the time of the eternal judgment. That will be the final judgment. In the New Testament we find that when Jesus was in this world in the flesh, He continually addressed words of condemnation to those who were on one particular side. This also appears in the Old Testament. Let's take another look at verse 29 of John chapter 5.

"And shall come forth; they that have done good, unto the resurrection of life; and they that have done evil, unto the resurrection of damnation."

You must be careful not to misunderstand this verse as meaning that you will go to heaven if you keep the law and live as a good person. The "good" referred to in this verse is the actions we perform through Jesus after we come to know the gospel. These are the deeds we carry out because we have come to know Jesus, the good deeds that make up a life lived for Him. Man cannot enter heaven on the strength of his own good works.

> Weeping will not save me ...
> Working will not save me ...
> Purest deeds that I can do, holiest thought and feelings too
> Cannot form my soul anew.[6]

Weeping will not save me. Working will not save me. Kind words or actions cannot bring about my salvation. In that case, what must I do?

Faith in Christ will save me![7]

"Faith in Christ will save me." It is a case of living by faith. Let's take another look at what is meant by good works.

> "For by grace are ye saved through faith; and that not of yourselves: it is the gift of God: Not of works, lest any man should boast. For we are his workmanship, created in Christ Jesus unto good works, which God hath before ordained that we should walk in them."
>
> Ephesians 2:8-10

We are "created in Christ Jesus unto good works." We are saved not as a result of our own works, but as a result of Jesus' good works. We live in order to reveal this truth on this earth.

> "Even when we were dead in sins, hath quickened us together with Christ, (by grace ye are saved;) And hath raised us up together, and made us sit together in heavenly places in Christ Jesus: That in the ages to come he might shew the exceeding riches of his grace in his kindness toward us through Christ Jesus."
>
> Ephesians 2:5-7

It says, "That in the ages to come he might show the exceeding riches of his grace." His grace has continued to be revealed from the time these words were recorded until now and so it is that we have come to know this gospel. So it is that the Bible says, "For by grace are ye saved through faith; … it is the gift of God: Not of works, lest any man should boast" Ephesians 2:8-9.

God has made it possible for all Christians to carry out good works in Christ as members of Christ's body. The Holy Spirit works within this body. As Christians, we need to understand that we are to have fellowship with one another and participate in the work of helping others to come to salvation.

16

Why Read the Bible?

John 5:30-47

The apostle John also said that John's Gospel was written
in order that we might receive eternal life.
If someone were to say that he had been digging beneath the rocks
in some valley deep in the mountains and had come across some gold,
everyone would rush there to dig.
But eternal life is so very precious
that perishable treasures such as silver and gold
do not come anywhere near it by comparison.

John 5:30-47

30I can of mine own self do nothing: as I hear, I judge; and my judgment is just; because I seek not mine own will, but the will of the Father which hath sent me. 31If I bear witness of myself, my witness is not true. 32There is another that beareth witness of me; and I know that the witness which he witnesseth of me is true. 33Ye sent unto John, and he bare witness unto the truth.

34But I receive not testimony from man: but these things I say, that ye might be saved. 35He was a burning and a shining light: and ye were willing for a season to rejoice in his light. 36But I have greater witness than that of John: for the works which the Father hath given me to finish, the same works that I do, bear witness of me that the Father hath sent me. 37And the Father himself, which hath sent me, hath borne witness of me. Ye have neither heard his voice at any time, nor seen his shape. 38And ye have not his word abiding in you: for whom he hath sent, him ye believe not.

39Search the scriptures; for in them ye think ye have eternal life: and they are they which testify of me.

40And ye will not come to me, that ye might have life. 41I receive not honour from men. 42But I know you, that ye have not the love of God in you.

43I am come in my Father's name, and ye receive me not: if another shall come in his own name, him ye will receive. 44How can ye believe, which receive honour one of another, and seek not the honour that cometh from God only?

45Do not think that I will accuse you to the Father: there is one that accuseth you, even Moses, in whom ye trust. 46For had ye believed Moses, ye would have believed me: for he wrote of me. 47But if ye believe not his writings, how shall ye believe my words?

The Will of the Father which Hath Sent Me

As I read the Bible, I wonder if any great speaker in the world has ever been more logical than Jesus was. There have been many orators in this world, and their logic and eloquence have rung in the ears of men and moved their hearts. There has never been anyone, however, who moved people's spirits, had such an impact on the spirit, or opened the eyes of the spirit as Jesus did.

The testimonies of those who have received the words of Jesus and proclaimed the gospel have also moved and brought about a change in the spirits of many others over the past two thousand years. Jesus' words were conveyed to His disciples, and since the coming of the Holy Spirit, those words have been proclaimed further through many other evangelists until the present day, so that we too have come to believe them. The above passage, from John chapter 5 verse 30 onwards, is Jesus' response to the heavy criticisms and attack that came upon Him for having healed the man who had lain sick for 38 years. The Jews paid no attention to the fact that Jesus had healed a man who had been ill for 38 years, and they made an issue instead of the matter of breaking the law of the Sabbath. Not only that, but they became even more resolved to put Jesus to death because He said that God was His Father.

At that time, Jesus was not simply offering a trivial defence against the attack of the Jews; the words He spoke apply even to us today. In the Gospels, we find that when Jesus prayed for the dead Lazarus, He said, "Because of the people which stand by I said it" John 11:42. Similarly, Jesus' response to the attack of the Jews when He healed this sick man contained words that prepared God's key to open the gates of the kingdom of heaven in advance for the spirits of all those who would need to come to know the gospel in later generations.

"I can of mine own self do nothing: as I hear, I judge: and my judgment is just; because I seek not mine own will, but the will of the Father which hath sent me." John 5:30

"I seek … the will of the Father which hath sent me." The One who sent Jesus was God. Jesus did not act according to His own wishes; everything He did corresponded to God's word. He was acting in accordance with the recorded word of God. Similarly, the prophets of Old Testament times always began their writings with phrases such as, "The word of the Lord came to me saying" or "Thus saith the Lord unto me." The prophets said that they were writing down the words that God had spoken. Now let's take a look at just how precisely Jesus acted in accordance with the words recorded by the prophets.

"And the glory of the Lord shall be revealed, and all flesh shall see it together: for the mouth of the Lord hath spoken it." Isaiah 40:5

This verse says that the glory of the Lord is revealed through Jesus.

"Behold, the Lord God will come with strong hand, and his arm shall rule for him: behold, his reward is with him, and his work before him. He shall feed his flock like a shepherd: he shall gather the lambs with his arm, and carry them in his bosom, and shall gently lead those that are with young." Isaiah 40:10-11

This shepherd is Jesus. There is a hymn that includes the line:

> Saviour, like a shepherd lead me.[1]

Jesus Himself said:

"I am the good shepherd: the good shepherd giveth his life for the sheep." John 10:11

These words of Jesus were neither humble nor arrogant. Since He truly was the good shepherd, He was merely stating a fact. A very clear blueprint of Jesus appears in the book of Isaiah. Once as I was reading through Isaiah, I was really astonished to realize that we have such a detailed explanation of the Christ laid out for us there and yet we carry on with our lives without knowing it! We are truly blind and we do not even know it! This is what I thought.

And With the Last; I am He

Let's take a look now at Jesus as He appears in a few passages in Isaiah.

> "To whom then will ye liken God? or what likeness will ye compare unto him? ... Have ye not known? have ye not heard? hath it not been told you from the beginning? have ye not understood from the foundations of the earth? ... To whom then will ye liken me, or shall I be equal? saith the Holy One." Isaiah 40:18, 21, 25

Here is a Person beyond comparison with any other. How can anything on earth possibly compare with Jesus?

> "Keep silence before me, O islands; and let the people renew their strength: let them come near; then let them speak: let us come near together to judment. Who raised up the righteous man from the east, called him to his foot, gave the nations before him, and made him rule over kings? he gave them as the dust to his sword, and as driven stubble to his bow. He pursued them, and passed safely; even by the way that he had not gone with his feet. Who hath wrought and done it, calling the generations from the beginning? I the Lord, the first, and with the last; I am he." Isaiah 41:1-4

The words, "Keep silence before me, O islands," call on the people of this world to humble their hearts. It is to the humble heart that Jesus appears.

> "The first shall say to Zion, Behold, behold them: and I will give to Jerusalem One that bringeth good tidings." Isaiah 41:27

The One who brings good tidings is Jesus. He came to Jerusalem and there He taught, proclaiming this message. Let's read through Isaiah chapter 42 from verse 1 and take a good look at who it is that appears here.

> "Behold my servant whom I uphold; mine elect, in whom my soul delighteth; I have put my spirit upon him: he shall bring forth judgment to the Gentiles. He shall not cry, nor lift up, nor cause his voice to be heard in the street. A bruised reed shall not break, and the smoking flax shall he not quench: he shall bring forth judgment unto truth. He shall not fail nor be discouraged, till he have set judgment in the earth; and the isles shall wait for his law. Thus saith God the Lord, he that created the heavens, and stretched them out; he that spread forth the earth, and that which cometh out of it; he that giveth breath unto the people upon it, and spirit to them that walk therein: I the Lord have called thee in righteousness, and will hold thine hand, and will keep thee, and give thee for a covenant of the people, for a light of the Gentiles; to open the blind eyes, to bring out the prisoners from the prison, and they that sit in darkness out of the prison house. I am the Lord: that is my name: and my glory will I not give to another, neither my praise to graven images. Behold the former things are come to pass, and new things do I declare: before they spring forth I tell you of them." Isaiah 42:1-9

These words present a portrait of Jesus. Here we can see how the Bible describes Jesus. Why did the Jews kill Jesus even though they were waiting for such a Christ to appear? Why did they have to kill Him even though they knew that a Messiah such as this would come? It was because they were not able to grasp God's word.

God, who commanded light to shine out of darkness, was intending to shine the brilliant light of Christ into their hearts,[2] but Satan veiled the spirits of those who did not believe. The Jews at the time of Jesus heard His words with their own ears, but their spirits were veiled so that they could not understand.

If we examine John chapter 5 from verse 30, we find that as Jesus spoke to those around Him of the eternal judgment that was to come, He made a black and white distinction between those amongst them who were qualified to believe and those who were not. He was explaining the difference between a person who believes and a person who does not.

My Witness

> "If I bear witness of myself, my witness is not true."   John 5:31

If Jesus had born witness of Himself, it would have held no weight at all. It could not have been real truth. The greatest witness to Jesus, however, is God's witness—the recorded word of God. That is why, when Jesus was tempted by the devil, He said, "It is written again, Thou shalt not tempt the Lord thy God" Matthew 4:7. Just as Jesus gave a warning against going beyond the recorded word of God, He Himself acted precisely in accordance with the words recorded in the Scriptures.

> "There is another that beareth witness of me; and I know that the witness which he witnesseth of me is true."   John 5:32

Jesus said He knew that the Old Testament scriptures that bore witness of Him were true. He did not bear witness of Himself; God the Father bore witness of Him. It was God who caused His word to be recorded in the Old Testament; His word that was revealed to man. Since Jesus was walking along the path that had already been recorded, this witness was true.

> "Ye sent unto John, and he bare witness unto the truth."   John 5:33

John the Baptist, who came to bear witness of the truth, was different from the one referred to as "another" in verse 32 where it says, "There is another that beareth witness of me." The testimony of John the Baptist was not God's testimony regarding Jesus. John the Baptist was not the truth itself. Jesus was the truth.

> "But I receive not testimony from man: but these things I say, that ye might be saved." John 5:34

"I receive not testimony from man." When Jesus said, "man," it included John the Baptist. John the Baptist predicted the coming of Jesus and pointed Him out when He came.

> "He was a burning and a shining light: and ye were willing for a season to rejoice in his light. But I have greater witness than that of John: for the works which the Father hath given me to finish, the same works that I do, bear witness of me, that the Father hath sent me." John 5:35-36

Jesus has a greater witness than that of John—the words of the Old Testament, which is God's witness. God the Father entrusted to Jesus the work that needed to be accomplished. The work Jesus carried out provided the evidence that demonstrated that He had been entrusted with God's word. This is why God said in the book of Isaiah, "Beside me there is no saviour."

> "Ye are my witnesses, saith the Lord, and my servant whom I have chosen; that ye may know and believe me, and understand that I am he: before me there was no God formed, neither shall there be after me. I, even I, am the Lord; and beside me there is no saviour. I have declared, and have saved, and I have shown, when there was no strange god among you: therefore ye are my witnesses, saith the Lord, that I am God. Yea, before the day was I am he; and there is none that can deliver out of my hand: I will work, and who shall let it?" Isaiah 43:10-12

God said, "Before me there was no God formed, neither shall there be after me." There is just one God and Creator. In this passage it says, "Ye are my witnesses, saith the Lord, and my servant whom I have chosen." The "witnesses" in this passage are the Israelites, the people who were chosen by the Lord God. As witnesses to the Old Testament, they brought it to completion. The history of the Israelites explains this.

Ye Shall Be Witnesses Unto Me Unto the Uttermost Part of the Earth

Once we come to believe in Jesus, we become His witnesses. What would happen if Jesus were different from God the Father? The Old Testament would have to be separated from the New Testament, and we would have to choose between believing in Jesus alone or in God alone. Let's consider now a verse from the book of Acts.

> "But ye shall receive power, after that the Holy Ghost is come upon you: and ye shall be witnesses unto me both in Jerusalem, and in all Judaea, and in Samaria, and unto the uttermost part of the earth."
>
> Acts 1:8

Jesus was not addressing these words to any particular individual, but to all Christians as a whole. The Holy Spirit came down at the time of the feast of Pentecost—ten days after Jesus ascended into heaven—and many people were filled with the Holy Spirit. After that, the gospel was spread throughout Jerusalem, the whole of Judea, Samaria, and now it has reached the ends of the earth. The words recorded by the apostles are being spread even to this day.

Just as the Old Testament was brought to completion within the history of the Jews who believed in the Lord God and acted according to His word, in New Testament times, the apostles made records of Jesus' crucifixion and completed the New Testament. So it was that Jesus spoke of the need for us to proclaim the truth in which we have come to believe.

"Ye are my witnesses ... and my servant whom I have chosen."

"But ye shall receive power, after that the Holy Ghost is come upon you: and ye shall be witnesses unto me both in Jerusalem, and in all Judaea, and in Samaria, and unto the uttermost part of the earth."

The Bible is the word of truth that proclaims Christ and bears witness of Him to all the nations of the world. God's promise recorded in the Old Testament—His promise to forgive all the misdeeds of the Jews—meant that when Jesus died on the cross, He took upon Himself the sins of all mankind. In addition, God's promise that He would not remember their sins also means that He has forgiven the sins of those who would become His children.

> "Remember ye not the former things, neither consider the things of old. Behold, I will do a new thing; now it shall spring forth; shall ye not know it? I will even make a way in the wilderness, and rivers in the desert." Isaiah 43:18-19

A new work begins in our spirits just like a river beginning to flow across dry land. God has promised to brighten and cleanse our hearts that were darkened with sin.

> "Thou hast bought me no sweet cane with money, neither hast thou filled me with the fat of thy sacrifices: but thou hast made me to serve with thy sins, thou hast wearied me with thine iniquities. I, even I, am he that blotteth out thy transgressions for mine own sake, and will not remember thy sins." Isaiah 43:24-25

God has said that for His own sake He will not remember our sins. If we are clinging onto our sins and suffering, we are also causing God to suffer. For His own benefit, God resolved to seek, through Jesus, all those who are lost in Adam. So it is that God tells us to trust in Him for everything.

> "Come unto me, all ye that labour and are heavy laden, and I will give you rest." Matthew 11:28

These words serve as a guarantee and promise that Jesus would bear the cross. Is anyone still burdened with anxiety, worries, and the load of his sin? "I, even I, am he that blotteth out thy transgressions for mine own sake, and will not remember thy sins." Isaiah 43:25 These words contain a tremendous blessing! Consider what must have been in God's heart as He said these words. Is there anything in which we can pride ourselves in the lives we have lived in this world? There is nothing except a heart that is grateful to God for the grace that He has bestowed on us. God sacrificed His only begotten Son in order to gain even just one more child for Himself. Jesus came to this earth as the Savior. "That was the true Light, which lighteth every man that cometh into the world." This light of heaven is a light that shines on each and every person. Why is it that people still do not come to understand the truth even though this holy light is shining?

> "But if our gospel be hid, it is hid to them that are lost: In whom the god of this world hath blinded the minds of them which believe not, lest the light of the glorious gospel of Christ, who is the image of God, should shine unto them." 2 Corinthians 4:3-4

This is because the light of the gospel is hid from them.

The Scriptures Are They which Testify of Me

> "And the Father himself, which hath sent me, hath borne witness of me. Ye have neither heard his voice at any time, nor seen his shape." John 5:37

"Ye have neither heard his voice at any time." But the Jews were listening to Jesus' voice. Whose voice was that? The voice of Jesus is the voice of God the Father. When Philip said, "Lord, shew us the Father," Jesus said, "He that hath seen me hath seen the Father; and how sayest thou then, Shew us the Father?"[3] The Jews had not seen God's physical form, but in actual fact, seeing Jesus was seeing God.

> "And ye have not his word abiding in you: for whom he hath sent, him ye believe not." John 5:38

"Ye have not his word abiding in you." This is because you do not believe the One that God has sent. If only the Jews had not just listened to the words of the Old Testament and forgotten right away what they had heard, when Jesus came in person and spoke and they heard His voice, they would have believed right away that He was the Christ. But the Jews did not know this.

> "Search the scriptures; for in them ye think ye have eternal life: and they are they which testify of me." John 5:39

In this verse, "scriptures" means the Old Testament. These Old Testament scriptures contain an account of everything about the Christ, from His birth to His death, and bear witness of Him. Through these Scriptures you can receive eternal life. The Jews read the Old Testament scriptures diligently, comparing one verse with another and researching them deeply, and they made all these efforts in order to receive eternal life. Their zeal was to be seen in the way in which they would write out verses and tie them to their hands or their fingers or attach them to the doorposts of their houses.[4]

"Of which salvation the prophets have inquired and searched diligently, who prophesied of the grace that should come unto you." 1 Peter 1:10 As it says in this verse, even as the prophets made a record of what the Holy Spirit told them, they examined and researched these Scriptures. The Bible tells us that they were looking for the grace that would come to us.

> "But these are written, that ye might believe that Jesus is the Christ, the Son of God; and that believing ye might have life through his name." John 20:31

The apostle John also said that John's Gospel was written in order that we might receive eternal life. If someone were to say that he had been digging beneath the rocks in some valley deep in the mountains and had come across some gold, everyone would rush there to dig. But eternal life is so very precious that perishable treasures such as silver and gold do not come anywhere near it by comparison.

> "For what shall it profit a man, if he shall gain the whole world, and lose his own soul?"   Mark 8:36

When it says here, "lose his own soul," it is not talking about losing the life of seventy years that we spend in the flesh in this world. It is saying that if a person loses eternal life, nothing else will be of any use to him.

> "And ye will not come to me, that ye might have life."   John 5:40

Jesus had said that the Scriptures bore witness of Him, but here He was telling them that even though they read the Scriptures, they did not think of coming to Him. Their physical bodies had come to Him, but their hearts were somewhere else. In other words, their hearts were not united with Him. These are words that can also apply to you. There are many people who attend church but only devote their mouths and their eyes to Jesus and not their hearts. Jesus said these words because He was distressed that such people did not come to Him.

I Am Come in My Father's Name, and Ye Receive Me Not

> "I receive not honour from men. But I know you, that ye have not the love of God in you."   John 5:41-42

If they had read the Old Testament scriptures, thought about them carefully, and been looking to see what kind of person was revealed there as the Christ, they would have been able to recognize Jesus. But people treated Jesus coldly. They did not glorify Him in the slightest. So Jesus promised that the Holy Spirit would come.

> "But the Comforter, which is the Holy Ghost, whom the Father will send in my name, he shall teach you all things, and bring all things to your remembrance, whatsoever I have said unto you." John 14:26

It was only after the Holy Spirit had come that people were truly able to recognize Jesus.

> "I am come in my Father's name, and ye receive me not: if another shall come in his own name, him ye will receive." John 5:43

Jesus explained this gently here, but actually these were important words that adorned a page of history. Jesus told His disciples that if people told them that the Christ is here, or the Christ is there, they were not to believe it.[5] He was warning them ahead of time that many false christs or false prophets would appear. Many false prophets have indeed appeared in the history of Israel. These words here in chapter 5 verse 43 are an important prophecy regarding an event that will occur in the future.

> "I am come in my Father's name, and ye receive me not: if another shall come in his own name, him ye will receive." John 5:43

Who is meant here by "another"?

Jesus foresaw that some day in the future when history on the surface of this earth is nearing its end, the gospel has been spread to the uttermost parts of the earth, and many people have come to know what sort of Person the Christ is, when the ideal and thoughts of a Christ are deeply embedded in people's minds, one person will appear promising perfect peace on this earth. As the antichrist, he will preach to mankind the message of peace on earth. But what is the peace that God promises us?

"Glory to God in the highest, And on earth peace among men with whom He is pleased." Luke 2:14—NASV

These are the words that the angels said to the shepherds when Jesus was born. If the words, "among men with whom He is pleased," were removed from this verse so that it said only "peace on earth," this would be a false peace. That would be a case of taking away some of God's word, and the Bible says, "And if any man shall take away from the words of the book of this prophecy, God shall take away his part out of the book of life, and out of the holy city, and from the things which are written in this book" Revelation 22:19.

"And on earth peace among men with whom He is pleased."

This is talking about the peace that comes to the heart of each individual.

"And they watched him, and sent forth spies, which should feign themselves just men, that they might take hold of his words, that so they might deliver him unto the power and authority of the governor. And they asked him, saying, Master, we know that thou sayest and teachest rightly, neither acceptest thou the person of any, but teachest the way of God truly." Luke 20:20-21

> Once Heaven seemed a far-off place,
> Till Jesus showed His smiling face;
> Now it's begun within my soul,
> 'Twill last while endless ages roll.[6]

> Peace! Peace! Wonderful peace,
> Coming down from the Father above!
> Sweep over my spirit forever, I pray,
> In fathomless billows of love.[7]

God wants this peace to dwell in our hearts and so He has proclaimed His heavenly glory and sent His only begotten Son into the world. He promised that peace would dwell in the hearts of those who accepted this only begotten Son.

Ye Seek Not the Honour that Cometh from God Only

> "I am come in my Father's name, and ye receive me not: if another shall come in his own name, him ye will receive." John 5:43

Some day, when people in many countries are waiting for the Christ, praying for His coming and believing that He will come, a person will appear claiming to be the only one who is able to accomplish peace on this earth. Someone will appear, revealing himself to the world through all the mass communications and claiming to be God. The apostle Paul wrote in advance about the appearing of this man.

> "Now we beseech you, brethren, by the coming of our Lord Jesus Christ, and by our gathering together unto him, That ye be not soon shaken in mind, or be troubled, neither by spirit, nor by word, nor by letter as from us, as that the day of Christ is at hand. Let no man deceive you by any means: for that day shall not come, except there come a falling away first, and that man of sin be revealed, the son of perdition; Who opposeth and exalteth himself above all that is called God, or that is worshipped; so that he as God sitteth in the temple of God, shewing himself that he is God. Remember ye not, that, when I was yet with you, I told you these things? And now ye know what withholdeth that he might be revealed in his time. For the mystery of iniquity doth already work: only he who now letteth will let, until he be taken out of the way. And then shall that Wicked be revealed, whom the Lord shall consume with the spirit of his mouth, and shall destroy with the brightness of his coming: Even him, whose coming is after the working of Satan with all power and signs and lying wonders, And with all deceivableness of unrighteousness in them that perish; because they received not the love of the truth, that they might be saved. And for this cause God

shall send them strong delusion, that they should believe a lie: That they all might be damned who believed not the truth, but had pleasure in unrighteousness." 2 Thessalonians 2:1-12

Someday the antichrist, the false christ, will appear before many people. This passage tells us that this incident will occur before Jesus returns to this earth. We need to know that this kind of person will appear as a deceiving spirit.

This is why Jesus said, "If another shall come in his own name, him ye will receive." Even now, the Jews as a state and a nation are waiting for the Messiah. They do not accept that Jesus who came two thousand years ago was the Messiah. In other words, they do not accept that He was the Christ.

"How can ye believe, which receive honour one of another, and seek not the honour that cometh from God only?" John 5:44

They preferred to receive honor from one another. In other words, they approved of one another when they were careful to abide by the law and offer sacrifices according to the law. Jesus was explaining man's true character as He pointed out that the Jews acknowledged one another, while flatly refusing to believe that He was the Son of God. Then in the end the Jews, thinking arrogantly that they knew the Scriptures, had the Christ nailed to the cross.

For He Wrote of Me

"Do not think that I will accuse you to the Father: there is one that accuseth you, even Moses, in whom ye trust." John 5:45

When the Jews criticized Jesus for breaking the law of the Sabbath, He said that God bore witness of Him as did the Scriptures. After explaining this to them, He then said that Moses would accuse them. He meant that the writings of Moses were already accusing them. What are the writings of Moses? They are the five books of Moses: Genesis, Exodus, Leviticus, Numbers, and Deuteronomy. Jesus was saying that even though the coming of the Messiah was promised in the writings of Moses, the Jews were intending to kill this Messiah which meant that they were ignoring Moses' promise.

> "The Lord thy God will raise up unto thee a Prophet from the midst of thee, of thy brethren, like unto me; unto him ye shall hearken."
> Deuteronomy 18:15

The "Prophet ... like unto me" of whom Moses spoke was the Messiah for whom the Jews had been waiting. They even asked John the Baptist, "Art thou that prophet?" This Prophet, however, is definitely Jesus Christ. This was the Word that appeared within the history of the Jews. The five books of Moses, including this book of Deuteronomy, did not come to an end with their being recorded at that time. Since these words continue to be proclaimed as long as the Israelites are living on this earth, they continue to be fulfilled, as Jesus said, "For verily I say unto you, Till heaven and earth pass, one jot or one tittle shall in no wise pass from the law, till all be fulfilled" Matthew 5:18.

> "I will raise them up a Prophet from among their brethren, like unto thee, and will put my words in his mouth; and he shall speak unto them all that I shall command him. And it shall come to pass, that whosoever will not hearken unto my words which he shall speak in my name, I will require it of him."
> Deuteronomy 18:18-19

What is the punishment that will be received by those who do not listen to Jesus' words? It is the punishment of going to hell. In any case, when the Jews killed Jesus, they would be ensnared by the commandment that says, "Thou shalt not kill." Who were they killing? They were killing the Messiah, the Christ, of whom it was written in the five books of Moses. In the Old Testament, there is a law that says, "Moreover ye shall take no satisfaction for the life of a murderer, which is guilty of death: but he shall be surely put to death" Numbers 35:31. The Jews killed Jesus and later in their history they had to pay a heavy price for it.

> "For had ye believed Moses, ye would have believed me: for he wrote of me." John 5:46

> "Moses wrote about me, so if you believed Moses, you would believe me." This is what Jesus was saying.

> "But if ye believe not his writings, how shall ye believe my words?" John 5:47

How did Jesus conclude what He was saying here? "You do not even believe the writings recorded by Moses, so how are you going to believe My words?" It is easier to believe something that is written down than to believe what is spoken, isn't it? Something that is written can be more easily understood than the spoken word. When you are listening, it is easy for the words you hear to be forgotten as soon as you hear them. Jesus was saying, "You don't even believe the recorded writings of Moses. How are you going to believe My spoken words?"

As Jesus explained His point in the process of this discussion with the Jews, He was not just tossing these words at people who had no hope as though pouring out water for people who had no container in which to catch it. Jesus was continually sowing the seed of the word in the hardened spirits of these people, in order that some time a shoot might sprout up. If you continue to read through John's Gospel, you will come to see how Jesus went about His work. Then at the end when Jesus hung on the cross and said, "It is finished," that was when perfect hope appeared.

Let us pray.

Holy Lord, we truly thank You. We were living aimlessly on this earth, but You came to this earth and, for the sake of our spirits, You took upon Yourself all the burdens that each of us carried in our hearts, and through Your forgiveness, You have made us children of God. We know that for as long as we live on this earth, we have been entrusted with Your word and You have given us the mission of participating in the work of bringing others to salvation and the knowledge of the love of God. Lord, we pray that You will strengthen each one of us so that our entire lives might be used in the furtherance of the work that You require to be carried out. We also pray that You will guide us so that we may participate in the kind of worship that is acceptable to You, and so that wherever Your name is heard there will be a continuation of the kind of work that glorifies Your name. We pray in the name of Jesus who was crucified and died out of His love for us. Amen.

♦ Notes

Chapter 8

[1] Indulgences were issued by the Roman Catholic Church during the late Middle Ages. They were vouchers stating that sins had been forgiven in return for money or goods donated to the church.

[2] See John 19:39-40.

[3] "Since Christ My Soul from Sin Set Free," Charles J. Butler.

[4] See Romans 15, 16.

[5] "Jerusalem, My Happy Home," Joseph Bromehead (1748-1826).

[6] "'Tis For You and Me," translated by John T. Underwood.

[7] "I'm Rejoicing Night and Day," Herbert Buffum (1879-1929).

[8] "A Wonderful Saviour Is Jesus My Lord," Fanny J. Crosby (1820-1915).

[9] "When All My Labours and Trials are O'er," Charles H. Gabriel (1856-1932).

[10] "Everything Is Changed," C. D. Martin (1866-1948).

[11] "The Love of God Is Greater Far" F. M. Lehman (1868-1953).

[12] "A Little Child May Know," Augustine (354-430).

[13] See Numbers 21:4-9.

[14] See also Mark 14:21.

Chapter 9

[1] "What a Wonderful Change," Rufus H. McDaniel (1850-1940).

[2] Charles Spurgeon, an evangelist from England (1834-1892). He was born again at the age of 15, he began preaching at the age of 16, and he played a major role in the gospel movement of his time.

[3] "Christ, Thy Lord is Waiting Now," S. F. L.

[4] According to the law, the price of a servant was thirty shekels of silver. Judas sold Jesus for thirty shekels of silver, meaning that he regarded Jesus as a servant. "If the ox shall push a manservant or a maidservant; he shall give unto their master thirty shekels of silver, and the ox shall be stoned." Exodus 21:32

[5] "Glory to Jesus Who Died," P. P. Bilhorn.

Notes

6 "The Love of God is Greater Far," F. M. Lehman (1868-1953).

7 "What Can Wash Away My Sin?" Robert Lowry (1826-1899).

8 "A New Name in Glory," Charles Austin Miles (1868-1946).

9 "Dying With Jesus," Daniel W. Whittle (1840-1901).

10 "River and Mountain, Streams Flowing Clear," Koong-Uk Nam (1862-1939).

11 "Come Home! Come Home," Ellen H. Gates (1835-1920).

12 See Luke 15:11-32.

13 The woman who had ten pieces of silver See Luke 15:8-10
Women at the time wore above their eyebrows a headband called "semedi". Some scholars say that it was an essential article in the marriage ceremony. In other words, they believe that the silver coins that women wore on the forehead or around the neck were their dowry.

14 See Luke 15:1-6.

15 "Sins of Years Are Wash'd Away," Anonymous.

16 "Walking In Sunlight," H. J. Zelley (1859-1942).

17 "I've Found a Friend," James G. Small (1817-1888).

18 "Go Forward," translated by John T. Underwood.

19 "The Trusting Heart to Jesus Clings," Eliza E. Hewitt (1851-1920).

20 "Pass Me Not, O Gentle Savior," Fanny J. Crosby (1820-1915).

21 "My Jesus, I Love Thee," William R. Featherstone (1846-1873).

22 "Once I Was Bound in the Grip of All My Sins," translated from Korean.

23 "Old Black Joe," Stephens Collins Foster.

24 "Once I Was Bound in the Grip of All My Sins," translated from Korean.

Chapter 10

1 "Weeping Will Not Save Me," Robert Lowry (1826-1899).

2 Baptism refers to a ceremony in which a believer who has been born again is fully immersed in water and then brought up out of the water to indicate that he has been buried and then risen with Jesus.

Chapter 11
[1] See 2 Kings 17:18-41.
[2] See Ezra 4:1-6.
[3] The Temple of the Samaritans
When Zerubbabel built the temple in Jerusalem, he considered the Samaritans as Gentiles and would not allow them to participate in the construction work. Later the Samaritans built their own temple on Mount Gerizim. This temple was destroyed in 128 B.C. by the Hasmonean king and chief priest, John Hyrcanus.
[4] "Fly as a Bird," Mary Stanley Shindler.

Chapter 12
[1] "Far Away in the Depths of My Spirit," Warren D. Cornell.
[2] "A Mighty Fortress Is Our God," Martin Luther (1483-1546).
[3] "In Fancy I Stood by the Shore, One Day," Lelia Naylor Morris (1862-1929).
[4] "My Hope Is Built on Nothing Less," Edward Mote (1797-1874).
[5] "O Happy Day, that Fixed My Choice," Philip Doddridge (1702-1751).
[6] "Far and Near the Fields are Teeming," James Oren Thompson (1834-1917).
[7] "Far and Near the Fields are Teeming," James Oren Thompson (1834-1917).
[8] "Hail to Brightness of Zion's Glad Morning," Thomas hastings (1784-1872).
[9] See Acts 9:1-5.

Chapter 13
[1] "Hail to the Brightness of Zion's Glad Morning," Thomas Hastings (1784-1872).
[2] "Come, Every Soul by Sin Oppressed," John Hart Stockton (1813-1877).
[3] "Encamped Along the Hills of Light," John Henry Yates (1837-1900).

Chapter 14
[1] The law forbade the Jews to do any work on the Sabbath day. In order to keep this law, the scholars of the law came up with detailed

particulars that were to be applied them to their everyday life.
2 NASV: Now there is in Jerusalem by the sheep gate.
NKJV: Now there is in Jerusalem by the Sheep Gate.
NIV: Now there is in Jerusalem near the Sheep Gate.
3 "Were You There When They Crucified My Lord?" African-American Spiritual.
4 See Matthew 12:8; Luke 6:5.
5 "What Can Wash Away My Sin," Robert Lowry (1826-1899).
6 See Genesis 3:13-15.
7 See Genesis 3:21.
8 "Since Christ My Soul From Sin Set Free," Charles J. Butler.
9 "What a Wonderful Change," Rufus Henry McDaniel (1850-1940).

Chapter 15
1 See Deuteronomy 8:3.
2 See Matthew chapter 9; Mark chapter 5; Luke chapter 8.
3 "I Know Not Why God's Wondrous Grace, Daniel Webster Whittle (1840-1901).
4 "Hail to the Brightness of Zion's Glad Morning," Thomas Hastings (1784-1872).
5 See Ephesians 2:4-5.
6 "Weeping Will Not Save Me," Robert Lowry (1829-1899).
7 "Weeping Will Not Save Me," Robert Lowry (1829-1899).

Chapter 16
1 "Saviour, Like a Shepherd Lead Me," Dorothy Ann Thrupp (1779-1847).
2 See 2 Corinthians 4:6.
3 See John 14:8-9.
4 See Deuteronomy 6:8-9.
5 Matthew 24:23; Mark 13:21.
6 "Since Christ My Soul from Sin Set Free," Charles J. Butler.
7 "Far Away in the Depths of My Spirit Tonight," Warren D. Cornell.